Little Plays for Little People

Little Plays for Little People
Theatre, Games, and Activities

Chari R. Greenberg

1996
TEACHER IDEAS PRESS
A Division of
Libraries Unlimited, Inc.
Englewood, Colorado

TEACHER IDEAS PRESS
A Division of
Libraries Unlimited, Inc.
P.O. Box 6633
Englewood, CO 80155-6633
1-800-237-6124

Production Editor: Susan Zernial
Design and Layout: Robert D. Getchell

Library of Congress Cataloging-in-Publication Data

Greenberg, Chari R.
    Little plays for little people : theatre, games, and activities /
Chari R. Greenberg.
    xi, 135 p. 22x28 cm.
    ISBN 1-56308-372-8
    1. Drama in education.   2. Play.   3. Children's plays, American.
I. Title.
PN3171.G78   1995
372.6'6--dc20
                                                    95-44205
                                                        CIP

This book is dedicated to my parents,
Harvey and Ellie Greenberg,
for all of their time and support.

Contents

Part 2
Plays for the Classroom

Preface

Playmaking theatre is an ideal way to introduce acting to students. What makes playmaking theatre unique is that no scripts are involved and the audience can be either classmates, other classes, parents, or all of these. Instead of using scripts, the narrator, usually the teacher, tells the story and feeds lines to students. With rehearsals, students can perform these plays and recite the lines with prompts from the narrator. Each play has a variable cast size to suit the number of students in the classroom.

Why use theatre in the classroom? It is a terrific form of expression that can be used as an educational tool. Theatre offers the opportunity for children to enter the world of make-believe, to become someone that they are not. Through acting, children develop public speaking skills, stimulate their imaginations, increase self-esteem and self-confidence, and have fun while doing it! Theatre benefits students in their individual growth as well as teaching them to work as a team. The best performances do not require an all-star cast but a cast whose members can support each other and work well together. Theatre in the classroom is a first step for students to learn acting skills, develop creativity, and appreciate teamwork.

The goal of this book is to assist teachers in using theatre in the classroom. In addition to the plays, theatre games and activities are discussed. Any of the theatre activities can be incorporated into lesson plans. I have taught theatre to children of all ages and feel confident that using theatre in the classroom is an excellent educational resource. Children need a form of expression, and acting offers them a vehicle to express themselves.

Acknowledgments

Over the years, I have been fortunate to learn from several talented people. Those responsible for my education in theatre have all been a part of the inspiration for this book. These people are Charlene Wanger, Debbie Stark, and Mike Lancy, Theater Department at Cherry Creek High School in Englewood, Colorado, Kevin Causey and Joel Silverman at Continental Divide Theatre Company in Boulder, Colorado, and Karen Romeo and Jeri Freidli at the Boulder Philharmonic in Boulder, Colorado.

Several schools and day care centers welcomed my theatre workshop and allowed me to hone each play. The directors at these centers were all encouraging and expressed to me how well this program worked at their centers. The children were the most inspirational. I watched them develop their acting skills more and more with each workshop and grow into more confident and creative actors. The centers and schools in the Denver and Boulder areas I would like to thank are Neighborhood Learning Center, Children's World, La Petite Academy, BMH Pre-School, Temple Sinai Pre-School, Happy Place Day Care Center, Toucan's Day Care Center, School Age Child Care at Coal Creek, Early Learning Center, and Children's Wonderland.

This book would not have been possible without the undying patience of my editor, Susan Zernial. I appreciate everything she has done to assist me in completing this book.

Also special thanks to my brother, Ari, for his encouragement, to my friends and family for their support, and to Wade Maslen. I will always be thankful to Wade for his patience, encouragement, understanding, and good ideas.

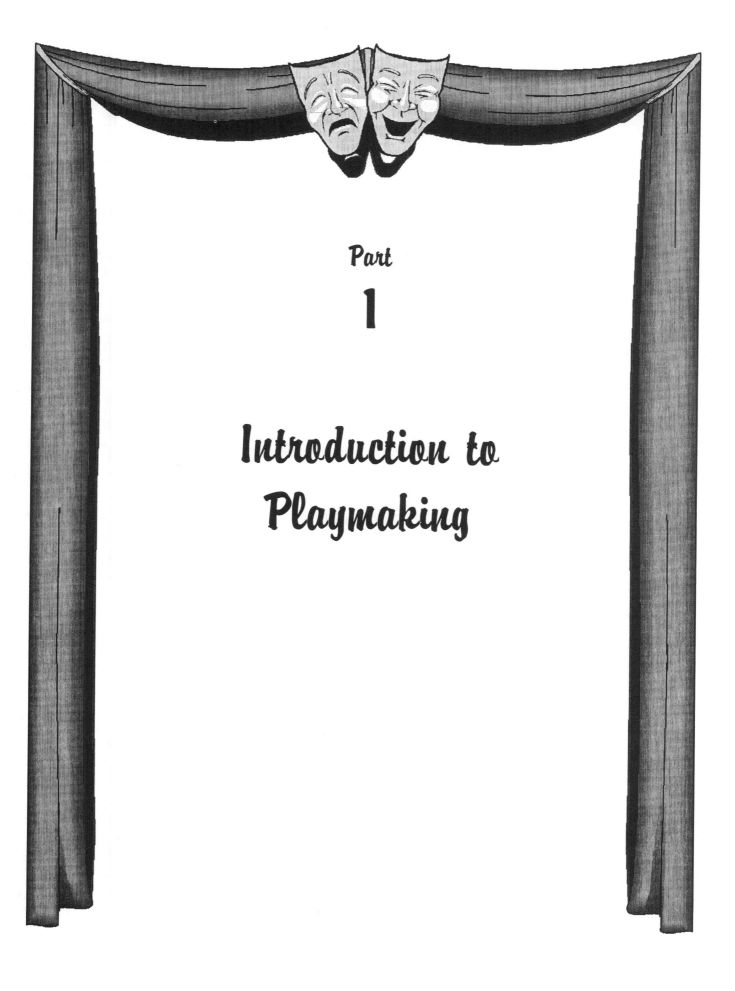

Part

1

Introduction to
Playmaking

1
How to Get Started

Acting for Young People

Acting is creating the illusion that you are someone other than yourself. Actors achieve this illusion by transforming themselves into characters. Some of the best actors are able to convince an audience of their characters by changing everything about themselves. Their voice, mannerisms, body language, walk, and body shape—all or only one may change to become the character. Others hardly have to change at all, because they are "typecast" into roles, which means the characters they are playing are similar to themselves. Teaching acting to young children should not be approached as producing another Hollywood star. Begin with the basic acting skills; teach young children how to change their voices, facial expressions, and walks to become different characters. Changing the voice, walk, and facial expression are easy qualities for a child to understand and relate to basic characters (e.g., how an old person speaks versus a baby). These should be reviewed every time you begin a theatre game or play.

Voice

The best way to teach your students about changing their voices is to give them examples. Using the phrase "I love acting," call on different students to change their voices to sound like the following characters:

> baby
>
> monster
>
> shy person
>
> very old person

Using the phrase "I love acting" for the four different characters should illustrate to your students how changing your voice can change whom you sound like. Ask students what changed about the voice with each character. Answers should be pitch (a high voice or a low deep voice) and dynamics (how loud or soft the voice was). Do some characters wrong; for example, talk to students like a baby and ask them if you sound like a very old person. Of course, the answer is you do not. Showing the difference between the right way to change your voice to match a character and the wrong way clearly defines how changing the voice is an important part of acting.

Walk

In acting, how you walk can let an audience know a lot about a character. Clear the room and have all the students stand on one side of the room, shoulder to shoulder. There should be enough room for them to walk across to the other side. Before beginning this exercise, show them an example of bad acting. Walk across the room briskly with a straight back and ask them if that is how a really old person would walk. Of course the answer is no, it is not how a really old person would walk. Ask them to tell you what you could do to convince them you are a really old person. Answers are walk slowly, bend your back, pretend you have a cane, and so on.

Call out the following emotions and types of characters and have students cross the room like those characters or persons with those emotions. For example, if you call out a sad person, they all cross the room in the way they believe someone sad would walk. Remind students that this is a game for how characters *walk*, not run. Instruct them to stop when they get to the other side of the room. When they have all crossed as sad persons, they wait for the next emotion or character and cross back. Use the example of an old person before they try it. Try some or all of the following characters and emotions:

angry	very old person
baby	sad
happy	scared
monster who walks slowly	spy (quiet and calculating)
nervous	superstar model or famous person

Encourage students who are having difficulty and compliment those who are doing a good job. Again, remind students that none of these are running exercises and each character should *walk* across the room.

Facial Expression

The face has many features that can be changed. The eyes, nose, and mouth can be widened or scrunched up, depending on the character. Read the following list of emotions to students. With students sitting, ask them to put on the face of each emotion. You might ask, "What does this emotion look like on your face?" Have them hold that emotion for about three seconds, then move on to the next one.

angry	mean
disgusted	sad
happy	scared
hurt	surprised

Conclusion

If there are more emotions or characters for the walks, faces, and voices you would like to use, feel free to add them to the list. Again, review the three changes—voice, walk, and facial expression—before doing any theatre activities or plays. It is important to continue to develop these skills in students so they can use them in plays and future theatre experiences.

2
Warm-up Theatre Activities

Before beginning a play, it is always a good idea to do some warm-up theatre activities. These activities allow students to become focused on theatre and are a great supplement to the plays in developing acting skills. The following activities are derived from my experiences in theatre classes, either as student or as teacher. The activities are "The Garden," "Statue Scenes," "Who Am I?" and "Special Guest."

The Garden

"The Garden" can be introduced by first asking students what grows in a garden. Once someone has answered flowers, get more specific. What kinds of flowers grow in a garden? Roses, tulips, daisies, irises, and so on. What is a flower before it becomes a flower? It is a seed! Ask students to find their own spaces and curl up on the floor as if they are seeds. This is your garden and all of the students are your flowers. The narration for "The Garden" is as follows:

"It's spring and I have just planted all of my seeds. I can't wait to see what my garden will look like this year. Oh, I think I need to water my garden. (Pretend to hold a watering can, walk around, and pretend to pour water on students.) This water should help my garden grow. Well, it's been a few days. I think my garden should at least start to grow now. I can see flowers coming up very slowly out of the ground. (Encourage students to very slowly start to stand.) Wow, I can't believe this garden; it's looking great. I think it needs some more water. (Go around and water all of the flowers again.) Well, that should've made some progress. I think I see my flowers growing some more. It looks like the stems are coming up out of the ground. (Flowers should be standing straight up, arms at their sides. Some students might stand up quickly. Remind them that this is a slow process.) Look at all of these flowers. They look great! I think I need to water them some more so that they will bloom. Flowers stay in one place because they don't have feet. (This is for those students who might move around. Repeat that flowers don't have feet and can't walk.) Here's some water for all you flowers. (Water the flowers again.) Oh my, I think I see some petals coming out. (Students raise their arms to be petals.) They all look so beautiful. (To a student:) What kind of flower are you? (Ask each student what kind of flower they are. If they take a long time to think of one, give them a suggestion.) What a great garden with so many types of flowers!

"But now it is summer and it is hot! It's so hot that you begin to wilt. (Show students how flowers wilt by leaning over just slightly.) I know what will help my wilting flowers—water! (Water the garden again.) As I water my flowers, they aren't wilting anymore. (Students stand straight up.) I guess I did not need to water my flowers because it looks like we're going to get a summer rain. It is raining hard and there is a wind blowing. (Flowers sway in the wind. Here you might need to remind students that flowers can't move their feet.) The rain storm is finally over, and the flowers are standing straight up with their petals high in the air.

"It's getting a little cold now because fall is here, and the petals begin to fall off of the flowers. (Flowers slowly put down their hands.) It gets colder and colder because now it is winter, and the flowers fall down into the ground. (Flowers curl up on the ground.) I can't wait until spring again. That was a great garden!"

"The Garden" can be played over and over, because each time you notice students becoming more and more detailed in how they hold their arms as petals, how they grow, and so on. "The Garden" is a great supplement activity to themes such as the Earth, plants and trees, and so on. "The Garden" is also a group activity; no stage and audience are needed because everybody is involved.

Statue Scenes

"Statue Scenes" is also a group activity. This activity gives students the opportunity not only to act, but to direct and learn how to work as a team. The goal of this game is to encourage creativity. First ask students, "What is a sculpture or a statue?" Usually a student answers that it is something that stands still. Then ask, "What can it be made out of?" The answers to this question are endless; examples include ice, metal, wood, plastic, and many others. The answer you are waiting for someone to give is clay. If no one says it, give hints so that someone thinks of it. Ask for two volunteers from the class to stand up and put their heads down. They are the clay and you are the sculptor. You are going to make them into a scene. For example, they could be playing baseball.

Move the students' arms and legs so that one appears to be holding a baseball bat and the other throwing the ball. The rules to "Sculpture Scenes" are the following:

> If you are clay, you cannot move on your own.

> If you are the sculptor, do not try to put your clay in a position they cannot hold (e.g., having a student stand on one leg).

> Respect each other and work together.

Before putting students into groups, make sure all students understand the rules listed above. Decide the groups and then assign each group its own space. Choose two students to be the sculptors and two to be the clay. Go to each group and give the sculptors a scene from the following list:

> bird-watching

> building a sand castle

> dancing

> getting a haircut

> going to dance class

> playing baseball

playing basketball

playing cards

running

studying

visiting the dentist

visiting the doctor

washing a car

watching a movie

You can add activities to the list or encourage students to think of their own. Have the students rotate the roles of the clay and the sculptors. This game is usually a group activity, but it can also be used as a performance. Each group can create its scene onstage while the other students watch. You can also use the same scene for each group. Stress to students to try to be different from the other groups. For example, group number one comes onstage and makes its clay into a dance class scene. One person might be the teacher and the other piece of clay might be the student. The second group comes onstage and also creates a dance scene for the audience. Except this time, both are students doing the same step.

Try variations of "Statue Scenes" to see which best suits your class. Remember, the object of the game is to encourage creativity. Students will develop the ability to think of scenes on their own and create their own masterpieces.

Who Am I?

"Who Am I?" is a game similar to the old favorite charades. In the context of acting, "Who Am I?" is an excellent game to allow students the opportunity to feel comfortable onstage and to develop skills in the three basic changes in acting. Ask all of your students to think of an animal. Each student comes onstage and acts out the animal, and the audience tries to guess what the animal is. You will find often that students come onstage and growl and that's all. When this happens, remind them of the three changes—voice, face, and walk. Does the animal they are acting out stand or crawl? How does this animal eat? Sleep? Does this animal have a scary face or a nice face? All of these questions should be asked while the students are onstage to encourage them to act out this animal to their full potential.

Many students will do the same animal as their classmates. It is perfectly acceptable to give them ideas before beginning the game. For example, animals that they could act out include a monkey, snake, cheetah, whale, and so on. If an animal has been acted out more than once, encourage students to think of an animal that has not been done. It is easy in this game for students to keep doing the same animals over and over. By doing the same animals, they do not really expand their acting abilities. By doing different animals, they are exposed to different facial expressions, mannerisms, and walks.

Special Guest

"Special Guest" offers students the opportunity to become their favorite cartoon character, TV or movie actor, or any other character they would like to be. For example, if students choose to be Bugs Bunny, they would walk across the stage like Bugs Bunny, sit down in a chair (center stage), and introduce themselves as Bugs Bunny. The audience asks questions, and it is Bugs Bunny's job to answer. The following is a list of rules for the game:

> Talk, sit, and act like your character.
>
> If you do not know the answer to a question, make it up.
>
> Audience should only ask appropriate questions.*
>
> Audience should treat the person onstage as if he or she is really the "Special Guest."

This is an acting exercise not only for the person onstage but for everyone. The audience must act as if the person onstage is a special guest. You need to be the judge if someone asks an appropriate question or not. Also, the person onstage is a guest; therefore, they do not know everyone's name. Take the example of the student who plays Bugs Bunny again. This student walks across the stage, sits down, and says, "What's up, Doc? I'm Bugs Bunny. What are your questions?" Students raise their hands to ask questions such as "Why do you like carrots so much?" "Where do you live?" and "Why do you play tricks on people?" You should ask questions as well. Many times your questions will inspire other questions from students. Allow from 5 to 10 questions to be asked of the "Special Guest." At the end, thank the guest for coming to visit your classroom today. All of the students should clap because it is the end of a performance, and the student onstage should take a bow.

Some of the characters I have seen students do are Bugs Bunny, the President, Tweetie Bird, Sylvester, Calvin or Hobbes, Janet Jackson, Garfield, Terminator, Ace Ventura, Barney, characters from the TV show *Full House*, Taz, a cowboy, a very old person, and a baby. Those are only some of the characters students can choose to do. Give the shier students suggestions to encourage them to go onstage.

Conclusion

All of these warm-up games can be played separately or together. They all give students a better understanding of acting and allow them the opportunity to become different characters. Always encourage students to change their voices, faces, and walks to become different characters. I suggest playing one or more of these games before performing the plays in the following chapters. Also, feel free to expand and vary any of the warm-up games.

---

*Questions that are appropriate are about the character. Inappropriate questions would be "Do you have a girlfriend or boyfriend?" or "What color is your hair?" Try to direct students to ask questions about the character or person. For example, if the person is an artist, one may ask, "What do you paint?" "What is your most famous painting?" and so on. Or if the guest is Tweetie Bird, one may ask, "Why do you dislike cats?" "Why do you play tricks on the cat?" and so on. Questions that are general and not directly related to the character should be avoided.

3
Friends 1 and 2

Friends 1 and 2 plays are a great intermediate step between theatre activities and playmaking theatre. Each play is a conflict and resolution situation, and all of the students perform at the same time. Students are in pairs, facing each other, sitting down cross-legged. You tell the story of Friends 1 and 2 and they act it out. Each story is about 15 minutes long, and these stories can be done with any size classroom. If you have an odd number of students, have one student be your assistant.

Before beginning each story, place the pairs in their own spaces, at least an arm's length away from other pairs. Students should also walk in place when the story instructs them to walk. Demonstrate walking in place so they understand they are not to begin walking around the classroom. For each pair, designate who is Friend 1 and who is Friend 2. Ask all of the Friend 1's to raise their hands, and repeat for Friend 2's. This is to make sure that students understand they can only be 1 or 2, not both.

To teach students how they will perform, make sure they understand that they repeat after you only if you say, "Friend 1 says, 'Let's go.' " Try the following example with your students:

Teacher: Friends 1 and 2 loved playing games together. They played cards. (All students should pretend to plays cards.) Friend 1 says, "This is fun!"

1: This is fun!

Teacher: Friend 2 says, "I agree."

2: I agree.

All of the 1's and 2's repeat after you at the same time. These short plays follow the same design as the plays in the following chapters. They are always performed with the student repeating the lines after you. Some students catch on quicker than others. To help students understand this format, I suggest doing the example above before performing each play.

Friends 1 and 2: The Fight

Students begin this play sitting cross-legged and facing each other.

Teacher: Once upon a time there were two friends. They loved to play games together. They would play checkers. (They pretend to play checkers.) They would play cards. (They pretend to play cards.) They would watch scary movies together and get really scared. They would watch sad movies together and get really sad. Sometimes they would cry. And they would watch funny movies together and laugh and laugh. One day, Friend 1 says, "Let's bake cookies."

1: Let's bake cookies.

Teacher: And Friend 2 says, "Good idea!"

2: Good idea!

Teacher: So, Friend 1 stands up (1's stand up) and says, "I'll get the flour and sugar."

1: I'll get the flour and sugar.

Teacher: Friend 1 walks over to a pretend pantry and gets the flour and sugar. They are both hard to carry, and they are heavy. Friend 1 puts them down in front of Friend 2. Friend 2 stands up and says, "I'll get the milk and eggs."

2: I'll get the milk and eggs.

Teacher: Friend 2 walks over to a pretend refrigerator and gets the milk and carefully gets the eggs. Friend 2 puts the eggs and milk in front of Friend 1 and says, "We need a mixing bowl."

2: We need a mixing bowl.

Teacher: Friend 2 goes to the pretend cabinet and gets a mixing bowl and brings it back to Friend 1. They both sit down together. Friend 1 pours in the flour while Friend 2 pours in the sugar. They both crack the eggs. And then Friend 1 pours in the milk. Friend 1 says, "We forgot the chocolate chips!"

1: We forgot the chocolate chips!

Teacher: Friend 1 goes to the pretend pantry and gets the chocolate chips. They both pour the whole bag in! Friend 2 says, "We forgot mixing spoons!"

2: We forgot mixing spoons!

Teacher: Friend 1 holds up both hands and says, "We can use our hands!"

1: We can use our hands!

Teacher: So they both mix up the cookie dough with their hands. They both lick their fingers. Friend 2 says, "Hmmmm, yum!"

2: Hmmmm, yum!

Teacher: Friend 2 says, "We need a cookie sheet."

2: We need a cookie sheet.

Teacher: Friend 2 gets a cookie sheet from the cupboard and brings it back to Friend 1. They both begin taking some cookie dough out of the bowl, rolling it into a ball, and putting it on the cookie sheet. They do it again, taking some cookie dough, rolling it into a ball, and putting it on the cookie sheet. They each do this 10 times. Let's count each cookie you make: 1-2-3-4-5-6-7-8-9-10! They both carefully lift the cookie sheet together, open the oven, and slide the cookie sheet in. They close the oven and they are done. Friend 1 suggests, "Let's draw while they bake."

1: Let's draw while they bake.

Teacher: Both of the friends begin to draw with markers. Friend 1 says, "I need that marker."

1: I need that marker.

Teacher: Friend 2 says, "Well, I'm using it."

2: Well, I'm using it.

Teacher: Friend 1 really wants that marker and says, "I need that marker now."

1: I need that marker now.

Teacher: Friend 2 refuses and says, "No!!"

2: No!!

Teacher: Friend 1 says, "Then I'm not your friend anymore."

1: Then I'm not your friend anymore.

Teacher: And Friend 1 turns his or her back to Friend 2 and folds his or her arms. Friend 1 is very mad, and his or her face looks very mad. Friend 2 says, "Well, that's fine."

2: Well, that's fine.

Teacher: Friend 2 turns his or her back to Friend 1 and folds his or her arms. They are sitting there, arms folded, back to back, and both feeling incredibly mad. After a while, they begin to look sad because they miss having fun. After a while longer, they realize they have been fighting over something silly. Friend 1 turns around and taps Friend 2 on the shoulder and says, "You know what?"

1: You know what?

Teacher: Friend 2 turns around and faces Friend 1 and says, "What?"

2: What?

Teacher: Friend 1 says, "I don't remember why we are fighting."

1: I don't remember why we are fighting.

Teacher: Friend 2 says, "Me neither."

2: Me neither.

Teacher: Friend 1 asks, "Can we be friends again?"

1: Can we be friends again?

Teacher: Friend 2 says, "Of course we can."

2: Of course we can.

Teacher: And they give each other a big hug. They both smell something really awful. It smells like burning cookies! They run over to the oven, put on the oven gloves, and quickly take the cookies out. Friend 1 turns the oven off. They pour themselves glasses of milk and eat the cookies. They were almost burned, but they got them out just in time. Friend 1 says, "These are delicious."

1: These are delicious.

Teacher: Friend 2 says, "I love them!"

2: I love them!

Teacher: And once again they are friends. They play checkers. (They pretend to play checkers.) They play cards. (They pretend to play cards.) They watch scary movies together and get really scared. They watch sad movies together and get really sad. Sometimes they cry. And they watch funny movies together and laugh and laugh. Friend 1 says, "I'm glad we're friends."

1: I'm glad we're friends.

Teacher: Friend 2 says, "Me, too."

2: Me, too.

The End

Friends 1 and 2: Patches

Teacher: Once there were two friends, and they were playing in a sandbox. They were making a sand castle. They dug into the sand and piled it high. There were towers, doors, and many other features on this castle. Friend 1 says, "This is fun!"

1: This is fun!

Teacher: Friend 2 says, "I agree."

2: I agree.

Teacher: So they continue to play. Just then they hear "meow." They both look up. Friend 1 asks, "What was that?"

1: What was that?

Teacher: Friend 2 says, "A cat."

2: A cat.

Teacher: They decide to keep building their castle because it is just a neighborhood cat. Higher and higher the castle grows. They have to stand up to keep building it. Then they hear it again. "Meow." Friend 2 says, "Let's go find the cat."

2: Let's go find the cat.

Teacher: Friend 1 brushes the sand off and says, "Let's go."

1: Let's go.

Teacher: They both brush and shake the sand off themselves and begin to walk. (Remind students to walk in place.) They look up in trees, and they look low under bushes. Then they hear it again. "Meow." Friend 1 says, "It sounds like it's over there."

1: It sounds like it's over there.

Teacher: They both walk over to a small cave. Friend 1 crouches down really low and slithers into the small opening. They hear it again, louder this time. "Meow." Friend 1 reaches inside the small cave and gently picks up a kitten. Friend 1 then slithers back out of the cave with the kitten. Friend 2 sees the kitten and says, "How cute."

2: How cute.

Teacher: Friend 1 says, "What should we name her?"

1: What should we name her?

Teacher: Friend 2 thinks about this and says, "How about Orange?"

2: How about Orange?

Teacher: Friend 1 says, "No, let's name her Brown."

1: No, let's name her Brown.

Teacher: Friend 2 says, "No."

2: No.

Teacher: So they both look at the kitten. She has brown and orange patches all over her. Friend 1 says, "I got it! Patches."

1: I got it! Patches.

Teacher: Friend 2 smiles and says, "That sounds great. Hello, Patches."

2: That sounds great. Hello, Patches.

Teacher: Friend 1 holds Patches while Friend 2 pets the kitten. Patches starts to meow. Friend 2 says, "I think Patches is cold."

2: I think Patches is cold.

Teacher: They head back to the playground with Patches. When they get there, they sit down together. Friend 2 said, "I'll go find a box for her to sleep in."

2: I'll go find a box for her to sleep in.

Teacher: Friend 2 stands up and goes all over the playground looking for a box. When Friend 2 finds one, they pick it up and carry it back to Friend 1 and Patches. Friend 1 puts Patches into the box and says, "We need something to keep her warm."

1: We need something to keep her warm.

Teacher: Friend 1 stands up and looks all over the playground for something to keep Patches warm. Finally, Friend 1 finds an old blanket under a bush. Crawling underneath the bush, Friend 1 pulls out the old blanket and shakes it to get it as clean as possible. Friend 1 goes back to Friend 2 and Patches. Friend 2 says, "That is perfect."

2: That is perfect.

Teacher: And they both lay the blanket in the box and pat it down. Patches curls up in the blanket and looks very happy. Friend 1 says, "I wonder if I could take Patches home."

1: I wonder if I could take Patches home.

Teacher: So, they walk home together (walking in place). They live near each other, and Friend 1 takes Patches home. The next day, when they see each other again, Friend 1 says, "My parents said I could keep her."

1: My parents said I could keep her.

Teacher: Friend 2 says, "Great, I'll help take care of her."

2: Great, I'll help take care of her.

Teacher: And the friends play together at the playground with Patches. They build sand castles that are huge, and Patches runs around them. They all become great friends.

The End

Friends 1 and 2: On a Walk

NOTE: Show students how to walk in place before beginning this story. Students will walk all over the classroom if you do not. It is important for each pair to know where its space is and stay in it.

Teacher: Once there were two friends going on a long walk together. They looked up into the sky and could see all the trees waving in the wind. The field they were walking through had tall grass, so they had to lift their legs really high with each step. (Show them how this is done, in place.) Friend 1 says, "It's beautiful out today."

1: It's beautiful out today.

Teacher: Friend 2 replies, "I love it out here!"

2: I love it out here!

Teacher: They continue walking with big steps. The grass gets shorter as they continue, so their steps get smaller. Friend 2 says, "Let's lie down here and cloud watch."

2: Let's lie down here and cloud watch.

Teacher: Friend 1 says, "OK."

1: OK.

Teacher: They both lie down on their backs looking up at the blue sky. There are clouds drifting across the sky. They look at the clouds and try to figure out what they look like. Friend 2 says, "I see a dragon."

2: I see a dragon.

Teacher: Friend 1 asks, "Where?"

1: Where?

Teacher: Friend 2 points into the sky and says, "There's his head, and he's breathing fire."

2: There's his head, and he's breathing fire.

Teacher: And they both study the dragon in the sky. Friend 1 says, "The dragon is becoming an elephant."

1: The dragon is becoming an elephant.

Teacher: And they both watch as the clouds change shapes. The dragon becomes an elephant with a long trunk. They keep pointing into the sky and saying the different animal shapes they can see in the clouds. (This is an opportunity for students to make up what they see. Just make sure the noise level does not get too high. Let them take a few moments to say what they see in the clouds.) After watching the clouds change for a while, Friend 2 suggests, "Let's walk some more."

2: Let's walk some more.

Teacher: Friend 1 stands up and says, "OK."

1: OK.

Teacher: Friend 2 stands up also. They both brush the grass off their clothes. They walk farther across the field until they come to a forest. They walk into the forest slowly. They can hear all kinds of birds chirping. Suddenly, they hear a hissing noise. Friend 1 says, "Don't move. It's a snake!"

1: Don't move. It's a snake!

Teacher: The snake slithers in front of them. Friend 2 says, "Don't be silly. Just walk around it."

2: Don't be silly. Just walk around it.

Teacher: So they carefully (in place) tiptoe around it. Friend 1 still looks pretty scared. Friend 2 says, "Look, it won't hurt you unless you try to hurt it."

2: Look, it won't hurt you unless you try to hurt it.

Teacher: Friend 1 thinks about that for a moment and then realizes that Friend 2 is right. Friend 1 says, "Let's climb that tree."

1: Let's climb that tree.

Teacher: Friend 2 nods yes, and they both begin to climb the tree. There are branches and twigs, and it is a huge tree. They keep climbing and climbing. But they are very careful to make sure that no one gets hurt. Friend 2 looks on one of the branches and says, "Hey, look what I found."

2: Hey, look what I found.

Teacher: Friend 1 climbs over to where Friend 2 is and looks. It is a bird nest filled with four eggs. Friend 1 reaches out to touch one of the eggs, but Friend 2 says, "Stop. Don't touch them."

2: Stop. Don't touch them.

Teacher: Friend 1 stops and just looks at the nest and eggs. The nest looks like a bunch of twigs and mud stuck together. The eggs are a dull yellow. One of them starts to move a little. Friend 1 says, "I think they're about to hatch."

1: I think they're about to hatch.

Teacher: They watch the egg slowly crack and crack some more. Finally, a little baby bird breaks out of the shell. It is so little. Friend 2 says, "It's a baby bird!"

2: It's a baby bird!

Teacher: They watch as the other three eggs began to break and crack, until all four baby birds are chirping their first chirps. Friend 2 looks and sees the mama bird coming. Friend 2 says, "Here comes the mom. We'd better go."

2: Here comes the mom. We'd better go.

Teacher: They both carefully climb down the tree. When they are down, Friend 1 says, "We'd better head home."

1: We'd better head home.

Teacher: Friend 2 says, "You're right. It's getting late."

2: You're right. It's getting late.

Teacher: They both walk toward the field with the tall grass. And they walk all the way home.

The End

Conclusion

These short plays can be used again and again. Each time you will notice students creating their own characters and improving their acting skills. It is also fun to do one of these plays before doing a full play because they involve everybody all of the time. Friends 1 and 2 have become a favorite in many of the classes I teach, and I am sure they will become a highlight for your students as well.

4
How to Use Playmaking Theatre in Your Classroom

Each play in this book includes an outline. The play outline contains important information for you to use before performing each play. The six sections in the play outline are the play synopsis, character descriptions, characters to use for auditions, sound effects, technical aspects, and suggestions. These sections are designed to make it as easy as possible for you to use playmaking theatre in your classroom, so make sure you read over each section carefully before doing the play in your classroom. The following is a description of each section and how it will assist you in doing any of the plays.

Play Synopsis

The play synopsis gives a basic summary of the play. This synopsis can also be used in a printed program if you are doing the play for parents or for any other kind of performance.

Character Descriptions

This section lists all the characters in the play and the characteristics of each part. In addition, it lists the ideal cast size and which parts may be eliminated or expanded, depending on the size of your class. It also offers suggestions for which type of student would best play each part. You can make a tentative cast list prior to class, based on what you know about your students and what is in the character descriptions. Always do the audition process before making a final decision on who should play which part.

Characters to Use for Auditions

This section lists the characters and lines to use for the audition process. Before defining this section, it is important for you to know about the audition process and how to know which students to cast in which parts.

Each play requires an audition process. Before auditioning students, explain what an audition is. Many students have tried out for sports teams, which make a great analogy to an audition. Auditions are tryouts in theatre to determine who will play what part. Also, it is important to let them know that just because they audition for a part, it does not mean that they will get that part. For example, in *Looking for Gold*, a student who auditions to be a pirate might be cast as a leprechaun. The audition is also an opportunity for you to determine which part will most benefit each student.

During the audition process, remind students not to just change their voices when auditioning. It is common for a student who is auditioning for a part, such as the evil wizard from *Looking for Gold*, to change only the voice. Encourage students to change their faces or how they stand, even to use their hands when auditioning. The audition process is a great time to apply the three changes—face, voice, and walk—to illustrate how those changes can make a character more believable.

Auditions should not take longer than 10 to 15 minutes. Each student should audition at least once. In each play, there is an "auditions" section that lists which characters to use for auditions. Before beginning, read the list of characters to the students to get them excited about all of the parts in the play. If possible, make mental notes about who is enthused about which parts as you slowly read the list of characters. When you begin the audition process, ask who would like to audition first.

How do you cast the parts? Every play is written so that each student, from the most outgoing to the most withdrawn, has the opportunity to participate. Auditions are also a chance to encourage shy children to come onstage. In my teaching, I have noticed that in a theatre setting there are three types of students: the shy child, the challenging child, and the natural actor.

The shy child is quite resistant to going onstage. A shy student can easily be identified as one who does not raise a hand to audition. This student should be asked to audition after several other students have already done so. If a shy student will not come onstage the first time you ask, encourage the student to just try any of the parts. If the student still resists, audition other students and ask the shy student again later. By this time, shy students should be willing to come onstage. When they do, if they giggle a lot or will not talk at all, cast them as a character that comes onstage with other students. For example, in *Goldilocks and the Many Bears*, these students could be flowers or animals.

Sometimes, shy students really come out of the shell once they are onstage. For example, in one class I taught, a seven-year-old boy would not come onstage. I asked him three different times throughout the audition process. Finally, he agreed to audition for Confused Bear from the play *Goldilocks and the Many Bears*. Once he was onstage, he was confident and outspoken and did a fantastic job. Even his teacher was surprised and commented that he was always shy in class. What he taught me was that even the most withdrawn student can be brought out of the shell through acting.

The challenging student might resist the idea of being in a play or demand the lead. Acting is a great form of expression for these students, who need to focus their energy in a creative process. These students generally enjoy playing the sinister characters in plays. When the list of characters is read, the challenging student's face will usually light up at the mention of an evil wizard, a mean lumberjack, or any other character portrayed as the "bad guy." You might even notice that if you audition these students to be the "bad guys," they not only use their voices to create their character but also change their stances and facial expressions. It is mainly these students who need to understand that they might not get the part they audition for. However, these students generally learn to love acting because it is a chance to be silly without getting into trouble.

In one school where I now teach regularly, the first time I was there one student questioned everything I said and was quite disruptive. But when I read the list of characters from the first play, *The Trees: The Lungs of the Planet*, he immediately wanted the role of the mean lumberjack. His audition was great, and I gave him the part. From that time on, he was not disruptive in the audience and was extremely respectful. His teacher said she wished he was like that all of the time.

The natural actor can play any role. Most students are natural actors, especially if you provide them with a strong foundation in the three basic changes—voice, walk, and facial expression. You will find in the audition process that most students are ready to come onstage and audition. With these students, you slowly nurture their acting skills and cast them into parts that will allow them to grow. There are also some natural actors who are extremely good and know it. These students often feel they should have the lead parts. Students need to be reminded that every part in a play is important, and if they can do a good acting job in this part, they can do other parts. Another important point to make is that good actors can do any part they are given. This could prove to be a good challenge for the student.

A story I tell students who are upset if they do not get a lead part comes from when I was in elementary school. We were doing a version of *Jack and the Beanstalk*, and I was cast as the back half of the cow. I was unhappy and disappointed, to say the least. But when the performance came, I made the best of it. I was determined to be the best back half of a cow ever and wagged my tail with my hand throughout the scene. I recall receiving lots of laughs for stealing the scene. The moral of the story is not to steal the scene, but to make the best of any part in which you are cast.

All types of students enjoy acting. There are just different ways to reach different students. Use the audition process to learn about your students, where their strengths and weaknesses lie. Through the acting games, auditions, and plays, your students will learn a lot about acting and have fun, and you will most certainly learn a lot about your students.

In the "characters to use for auditions" section of each play, characters from that play are listed to use for auditions. Each student should audition at least once while you make notes on the audition worksheet. It is a good idea to list on the audition worksheet at least two characters that each students could play, and then cast the play from that list. Sometimes there is a student who is perfect for a part. In that case, circle the part on the audition worksheet so you know the part is filled. For example, auditioning a student for *Looking for Gold* might go like this:

The teacher asks Jenny to audition for the part of a pirate. Jenny stands center stage and waits for the line from the teacher. The teacher asks Jenny, "How does a pirate stand? What does a pirate's face look like?" Then the teacher gives her the line to say. "Pirates say, 'Hey there, Matey!' " And Jenny repeats, "Hey there, Matey." Then the teacher auditions the next student.

Each play provides at least three characters to use for auditions. Rotate the characters you use. Maybe the first student will audition for a pirate, the second for a leprechaun, the third for the Evil One, and so on. During this time, repeat to students that they will not necessarily get the part they audition for.

The audition worksheet is designed for you to keep a record of whom to cast in which part. This worksheet appears on a separate page in each play, so you may copy it as many times as necessary. The following sample audition sheet is based on a class of 25 students doing the play *Looking for Gold.*

*Sample
Audition
Worksheet*

Sara: Katie, Rose, Susie, Jenny, Kelsey

Jim: Josh, Rob, Chris, Justin, Jeremy

Magic Wizard: Heather, Nina, Lisa, Gayle, Brandon

Evil One: John, Tom, Heather, Lisa, Tory

Sidekick: Allie, Nina, Katie, Tom, Kyle, Tyler

Captain Pirate: Rob, Josh, Alisa, Breda, Laura

Parrot: Tory, Gayle, Nicole, Kyle, Kelsey, Jeremy

Gold: Jenny, Laura, Kelsey

Leprechauns: John, Jenny, Justin, Jeremy, Breda, Allie, Rose

Pirates: Nicole, Susie, Chris, Laura, Brandon, Tyler

After auditioning all the students, make the final cast list. Cross off or check off each character as you cast the part. The final cast list may be posted in the classroom or kept for your own records. The final cast list also appears on a separate page, so you may copy it as many times as needed. I suggest doing each play several times and allowing students to play different characters each time. The sample final cast list appears on the following page.

As you cast the play, you will notice that the parts that can have 1 to 10 students are always cast last. The reason for this is to include all students in the play. For example, in *Looking for Gold*, there would be 18 students left from a class of 25 after you have cast the main characters. The rest will be pirates and leprechauns. Ask students who do not have a part to raise their hands. As you write down their names, write down which part they are until all students are cast in the play.

Once the cast list is complete, different plays have different portions to rehearse before beginning. For example, in *Goldilocks and the Many Bears*, the bears rehearse their lines before the play is performed. Be sure to read this section carefully and make sure your students rehearse the necessary lines prior to performance.

Sound Effects

Most sound effects in the plays should also be reviewed before doing a play. Each play has its own set of sound effects that the audience makes. This section lists the sound effects to practice and those that do not need to be practiced but are in the play. Practice the sound effects by telling students, "You will be doing the sound effects for this play. What does a breeze sound like?" Students create the breeze sound effect. Also, it is important to practice how to stop the sound effect. When you are ready to move on to the next sound effect, do not tell students to stop. Instead, use your hand to make a stop motion. Instruct students to watch your signals for when to start and when to stop. Hand motions are generally used to start and stop, because when the sound effect takes place, the teacher is busy narrating the story and cannot use the voice to instruct students.

The breeze sound effect is common in plays. As an example of how the sound effect is incorporated into a play, the narration reads, "A breeze began to blow." Use your hand motion for the students to begin the sound effect. Let them enjoy creating the breeze for a brief interval, then use the hand motion for them to stop. After they have stopped, continue performing the play.

Sometimes students forget to do the sound effect. It is fine to remind students about the sound effect. For example, in *The Trees: The Lungs of the Planet*, there is a watering-the-trees sound effect. The narrator says, "And the planters watered the trees." Give students a chance to do the sound effect and pause. If they do not do it, remind them: "I don't hear the sound of watering trees." After doing the plays a few times, students learn when to do sound effects. It is a great way for them to improve their listening skills and be actively involved in the play, even when they are in the audience. Sound effects are an opportunity for students to make noise without getting into trouble.

Sample Final Cast List

Sara: Katie

Jim: Rob

Magic Wizard: Lisa

Evil One: Tom

Sidekick: Tyler

Captain Pirate: Breda

Parrot: Tory

Gold: Kelsey

Leprechauns: John, Jenny, Justin, Jeremy, Allie, Rose, Heather, Alisa, Gayle

Pirates: Kyle, Nicole, Susie, Chris, Laura, Brandon, Nina, Josh, Rob

Technical Aspects

This section includes any props (a prop is anything handheld in a play), set pieces (e.g., chairs, table, etc.), costumes, or any other items needed for the play. Many props and costumes are optional, depending on whether the play is a performance for parents or only used as an acting exercise in the classroom.

Suggestions

Suggestions or comments are in this section, which provides any further information about the play that is not listed in the prior sections.

Conclusion

All of the sections described above are designed to assist you in performing playmaking theatre. As the narrator, you, too, play an important role in each play. Because the students repeat the lines in each play after the narrator, it is important to speak the line as it should be acted. If you recite a line in a monotone, chances are the students will repeat it that way. Initially, how students speak onstage will be up to you and the way you say the line first. For example, in *The Trees: The Lungs of the Planet*, the lumberjack is out of breath at the end and can hardly speak. When you say this line, you will find that if you do not sound out of breath, neither will the lumberjack. Eventually, students will begin to form their own voices for the characters and will not necessarily imitate you. But in the beginning, it is important to help them develop those acting skills by saying lines as the character would.

It is important that students learn that being in the audience is just as important as being onstage. There are two audience rules I use in my classes: Sit cross-legged with hands in your lap, and do not talk during the performance. Review these audience rules with your class before doing any theatre activities or plays. When students get noisy during any of the plays or activities, remind them to observe the audience rules.

One great advantage of using playmaking theatre is that no memorization is required for students. This comes in handy if you use any of the plays for performances for parents or other classes. The pressure is off the students to remember where to stand or what their lines are. It has been my experience that at least one student will get stage fright. In this scenario, simply recast the part with someone else. There are no lines to relearn or any pressure on you to find a way to fill that part.

During the performance, students are not to wait offstage for their entrances. Instead, they are all seated at the foot of the stage, participating in the sound effects. Having them there rather than offstage keeps them involved in the performance the entire time. As the narrator, you should be on one side of the stage at all times. It is perfectly acceptable to use the book as you tell the story. Memorization is not necessary.

Be sure to read the play outline before each play. It contains information that is needed to perform each play to its full potential. Each play has different sound effects, characters, and special notes. Each play also provides the lines that the student should repeat after you. Remember, playmaking theatre is an exercise in acting, not reading. It is designed to give students the freedom to act. By reading through each section carefully, you can become familiar with the play and all its requirements.

Part

2

Plays for
the Classroom

5
Goldilocks and the Many Bears

Play Synopsis

Goldilocks and the Many Bears is a new version of the favorite story "Goldilocks and the Three Bears." In this new version, there are Rappin' Bear, Complaining Bear, Confused Bear, and Excited Bear. Goldilocks loses her way in the forest, and deer, rabbits, and birds try to help her. Finally, she finds a cottage where she eats and rests. The bears come home to discover a stranger asleep in their cottage. When she awakens, she realizes the bears are nice bears, and they offer to help her find her way home.

Character Descriptions

Cast size: An ideal cast size is from 16 to 19 students. If your class is smaller, have just one flower, one deer, one rabbit, and one bird, or have three or four students play all four parts (cast size of 9 to 10 students). If your class is larger, increase the number of students who play the animals and have two or three students play the flowers.

Goldilocks is an expressive child. This part is best played by a student who has good speaking skills and the ability to follow directions. Goldilocks is onstage the entire play. Goldilocks does not have to be a blonde. I have also had male students play Goldilocks, and they were great!

Rappin' Bear is very cool. This character always has a calm manner. Your "class clown" usually plays this part well.

Complaining Bear is never happy with anything. Everything is always too much or too little. Best played by a student who really does complain a lot, it is a great outlet for this type of personality.

Confused Bear is very comical. This character does not understand anything that is going on. Audition some of your quiet or shy students for this part—they may surprise you!

Excited Bear is always happy. This bear loves everything and is extremely outgoing. Best played by a student who is very enthusiastic and likes to jump up and down.

Rabbits, deer, and birds are animals in the forest. They all try to help Goldilocks find her way home. These parts can be played by from one to five students for each animal. Cast these parts after you have cast Goldilocks and the bears. Ask students which animal they would like to play, and have each group sit together (i.e., rabbits all sit in the front, deer in the second row, and birds in the third row).

Flowers stand tall and proudly with their petals (arms) in the air. Best played by the shy and quiet students who will not come onstage for an audition, or, if they do, who can hardly be heard.

Characters to Use for Auditions

Have each student audition at least once. Characters to use for auditions are the following:

Rappin' Bear says, "It's cool."

Complaining Bear says, "It's too hot! It's too cold!"

Confused Bear scratches (his or her) head and says, "I don't understand."

Excited Bear jumps up and down and says, "What a great day!"

Copy the audition worksheet and final cast list on the next two pages as many times as needed.

Goldilocks

Rappin' Bear

Complaining Bear

Confused Bear

Excited Bear

Deer

Rabbits

Birds

Flowers

Notes or comments:

Final Cast List

Goldilocks

Rappin' Bear

Complaining Bear

Confused Bear

Excited Bear

Deer

Rabbits

Birds

Flowers

Notes or comments:

Cast the parts of the bears and Goldilocks first. Choose Rappin' Bear and have that character sit in the first chair. Teach the student Rappin' Bear's line by using the prompt "Rappin' Bear folds (his or her) arms and says." At that point, Rappin' Bear should say the line, "It's cool." Then cast the part of Complaining Bear and do the same to teach Complaining Bear's line. Repeat this for Confused Bear and Excited Bear. After all the bears are cast and onstage, review their lines with them. Then have them sit together in the audience. Next, cast the part of Goldilocks and have Goldilocks come onstage. And last, cast the parts of the animals and flowers. Ask the students which they would like to be, then group them so the rabbits are sitting with the rabbits, deer sitting with deer, and so on.

Sound Effects

Before beginning the play, practice the following sound effects with students two or three times:

> a breeze

> forest animal noises

Practice the hand motions to start and stop the sound effects. (Refer to the audition section of the book, chapter 4.)

When Goldilocks says, "This is perfect," the audience claps. (This is when she is in the cottage.)

Other sound effects that are in the script but do not need to be practiced include stomach growling, eating fast, yawning, and snoring.

Technical Aspects

The stage should have three chairs arranged in this way:

Chair 1 is for Excited Bear, chair 2 for Complaining Bear, and chair 3 for Rappin' Bear. The space between chair 1 and chair 2 is where Confused Bear stands. The space labeled "Goldilocks sleeps" is where the last pretend bed that Goldilocks tries should be, past the chairs.

Props: Bowls and spoons are optional. Goldilocks can pretend to be holding these items.

Suggestions

Goldilocks and the Many Bears is a great play to do when you have been reading any of the classic fairy tales to students. Most children are familiar with the original version of this tale and enjoy acting out this variation. If you do this play for a performance, here are some costume suggestions: Deer, rabbits, and birds can wear headbands with the respective animals' ears on top. Or use sandwich boards to write what animal they are. The bears can wear brown mittens and bear ears and noses made of construction paper or felt.

Goldilocks and the Many Bears: The Play

Teacher: Once upon a time there was a girl named Goldilocks. She loved to go on walks. One day she was on a walk through the forest. (Goldilocks should walk in place.) She looked at all of the trees around her and the clear skies and said, "What a beautiful day."

Goldilocks: What a beautiful day.

Teacher: She continued to walk through the forest. She looked up into the sky and squinted her eyes because the sun was so bright. (Goldilocks squints her eyes.) She took a deep breath of the fresh air that surrounded her. Along her path, she saw some flowers. (Flowers come onstage and stand to the left of Goldilocks. All of the flowers should have their arms in the air like petals.) Goldilocks said, "What pretty flowers."

Goldilocks: What pretty flowers.

Teacher: Then she said, "I think I'll pick them."

Goldilocks: I think I'll pick them.

Teacher: So Goldilocks walked over to the flowers and started to pick one of them. (Motion to Goldilocks to pick the flowers from their ankles.) But just as she was about to pull one of the flowers from the ground, it shouted, "Ouch!"

Flower: Ouch!

Teacher: And Goldilocks jumped back and covered her mouth in surprise. "I'm sorry," she said.

Goldilocks: I'm sorry.

Teacher: And all of the flowers said, "Don't pick us!"

Flowers: Don't pick us!

Lumberjack: All right!

Teacher: Lumberjack said, "I love trees."

Lumberjack: I love trees.

Teacher: And everyone clapped, and Lumberjack did not chop down any more trees.

The End

7
Looking for Gold

Play Synopsis

Looking for Gold takes students on a journey with Sara and Jim to find "Gold." A Magic Wizard helps them, but leprechauns, pirates, and an Evil One try to reach Gold before Sara and Jim do. In the end, the audience members learn to their surprise that "Gold" is a friend of Sara and Jim, a true treasure.

Character Descriptions

Cast size: An ideal cast size is 15 to 20 students. If your class is smaller, you can cut the Sidekick, Parrot, and extra pirate. If your class is large, you can have several pirates and leprechauns. Also, you can add Silver, making the story *Looking for Silver and Gold.*

Sara and Jim are good friends who want to find their friend Gold. They do not understand why everyone is making such a fuss over the map that they carry. Both are strong characters and should be played by students who are outgoing and confident onstage.

Gold is told secretly of (his or her) part. The first time that students perform the play, only Gold will know what the treasure really is. Gold should be played by a student who can keep a secret.

Magic Wizard is wise. This part should be played by a student who is articulate and who can jump onstage fast. The Magic Wizard seems to know all and protects Sara and Jim. Whoever is cast as the Magic Wizard should make up some magic words and remember them. They will be spoken later in the play.

Evil One is a sinister character, best played by a student who has dominant characteristics. The Evil One is feared by Sara and Jim. Whoever is cast as the Evil One should make up some magic words and remember them. They will spoken later in the play.

Sidekick is the assistant to the Evil One.

Captain Pirate is much feared by Sara and Jim. This character is loud and intimidating.

Parrot repeats everything the Captain says. The student playing Parrot flaps arms like wings.

Pirates should all be mean characters. Some may have one eye missing. There should be at least one extra pirate.

Leprechauns love to dance. Each one has a funny little dance to do. There should be at least two leprechauns.

Characters to Use for Auditions

Have each student audition at least once. Characters to use for auditions are the following:

The Evil One says, "I want Gold!" and then laughs an evil laugh.

A pirate says, "Hey there, matey."

A leprechaun says, "Try to catch me if you can."

While auditioning each student, make notes about who is strong onstage and who is not. Everyone should have a part in this play. The students who are strong onstage should have the lead parts; other students should be cast as pirates or leprechauns. Use a pencil on the list of characters on the audition worksheet to cast the parts while you audition students.

Audition Worksheet

Sara

Jim

Magic Wizard

Evil One

Sidekick

Captain Pirate

Parrot

Leprechauns (at least one)

Pirates (at least one)

Gold

Notes and comments:

Final Cast List

Sara

Jim

Magic Wizard

Evil One

Sidekick

Captain Pirate

Parrot

Leprechauns

Pirates

Gold

Notes and comments:

Once you have decided who Gold will be, tell that student the part in secret. Explain that no one else is to know and that the student should sit near you until it is time to go onstage. Let the other students know that this person's part is a secret that they will discover at the end. After you have cast Sara and Jim, bring them both onstage and have them repeat after you the following lines:

Sara: Which way to Pirate Bridge?

Jim: I don't know.

This is to make sure they work well together and can repeat after you with no problem. Then bring the Evil One and Sidekick onstage and have them repeat after you the following lines:

Evil One: I want Gold!

Sidekick: (She or he) wants Gold.

The Evil One and Sidekick should sit together in the audience. And last, bring the Parrot and Captain Pirate onstage. They repeat after you the following:

Captain: Hey there, matey.

Parrot: (Squawk) Hey there, matey.

Encourage all of the students to make facial expressions and to change how they stand and how they talk. Remind them that all of these changes are a part of acting. Finish casting the remaining students, and have all of the pirates sit together and the leprechauns all sit together in the audience.

Bring all the leprechauns onstage and have them make a circle around Sara and Jim. Explain to them that when they come onstage in the play, they should make a circle right away and start dancing around Sara and Jim. In addition, tell Sara and Jim that they are not to try to catch the leprechauns but only to look confused.

Sound Effects

Now that all of the students know their parts, teach them the sound effects. First, tell them that throughout the play you will need their help making sound effects. Second, go through each of the following sound effects with them:

When the Magic Wizard appears, the audience says, "Poof!" Have the Magic Wizard jump onstage as the audience says, "Poof!" Then the Magic Wizard disappears, and the audience again says, "Poof!" And the Magic Wizard jumps back into the audience. Rehearse this two or three times with the class.

Have the students make a breeze sound. Motion to them with your hand to stop. Practice this until most of the students stop the breeze noise when you do the hand motion to stop.

Forest animal noises should include birds, wolves, owls, snakes, and so on. Practice the same way as with the breeze sound.

When the Evil One and Sidekick come onstage, the audience boos and hisses. Again, use the stop hand motion for the students to stop making the sound effect.

Technical Aspects

You will need a small stage and a large enough space for the students to sit in an audience. The only prop needed is a piece of paper for a map. The Magic Wizard should have this map at the beginning of the play.

Suggestions

Looking for Gold is a great story to do when your theme of the week is friendship. This can also be rehearsed for a parents' night performance. For costumes, students can make hats for their characters (green hats for leprechauns, black hats for pirates, etc.). It is not repetitious to do the story more than once, with students trying different parts each time. The more familiar they become with the story, the less the narration will be needed. Remember, the goal of playmaking theatre is to introduce acting to your students. The more they practice the play, the more their acting skills will develop.

Looking for Gold: The Play

Teacher: Once there were two friends, Sara and Jim. And Sara said, "I wonder where we can find Gold?"

Sara: I wonder where we can find Gold?

Teacher: Jim said, "I don't know."

Jim: I don't know.

Teacher: Suddenly, a Magic Wizard appeared. (Magic Wizard jumps onstage. Audience says, "Poof!")

Teacher: Magic Wizard looked very wise. Sara and Jim looked surprised to see a Magic Wizard. Magic Wizard asked, "Are you looking for Gold?"

Magic Wizard: Are you looking for Gold?

Teacher: Sara said, "Yes, we are."

Sara: Yes, we are.

Teacher: Jim asked, "Can you help us?"

Jim: Can you help us?

Teacher: Magic Wizard paused for a moment to think. And then (he or she) said, "Yes, I can."

Magic Wizard: Yes, I can.

Teacher: Magic Wizard pulled a map out of (his or her) sleeve. Sara and Jim got excited about finding Gold. Magic Wizard handed Sara the map and said, "Here is a map to help you find Gold."

Magic Wizard: Here is a map to help you find Gold.

69

Teacher: Magic Wizard folded (his or her) arms and looked wise. (He or she) warned them both, "Be very careful."

Magic Wizard: Be very careful.

Teacher: And Sara and Jim both nodded their heads and said, "We will, thank you."

Sara and Jim: We will, thank you.

Teacher: And then Magic Wizard disappeared. (Audience says, "Poof!") Jim and Sara looked at that map to decide which way to go. The map was filled with lots of different places to go. They were not sure which way to go first. Finally, Jim pointed to the map and said, "It looks like we go through the green forest first."

Jim: It looks like we go through the green forest first.

Teacher: Sara looked at the map closely and pointed straight ahead and said, "I think it's over that way."

Sara: I think it's over that way.

Teacher: Jim and Sara began to walk (in place) toward the green forest. Sara asked Jim, "Have you ever been in the green forest?"

Sara: Have you ever been in the green forest?

Teacher: And Jim shook his head and said, "No, but it sounds like an adventure."

Jim: No, but it sounds like an adventure.

Teacher: As they got closer, they could hear a slight breeze (audience makes breeze sound effect). As they came to the green forest, Jim and Sara looked at the gigantic trees in front of them. They began to walk into the green forest. The bushes and trees were so thick they had to use their hands and arms to push them out of the way. There was hardly any room to walk. As they went deeper and deeper into the green forest, they heard the forest animals making noises. (Audience makes forest animal noises.) Jim timidly asked, "What was that?"

Jim: What was that?

Teacher: Sara replied, "I don't know, and I don't want to know."

Sara: I don't know, and I don't want to know.

Teacher: They continued to walk through the green forest. The farther they got into the forest, they found there weren't as many trees and bushes to move out of the way. It was actually quite a beautiful place. Suddenly leprechauns appeared and began dancing around them. (Leprechauns make a circle around Sara and Jim.) Sara and Jim looked confused because they did not know who the leprechauns were or what they were doing. The leprechauns began chanting, "Try to catch me if you can."

Leprechauns: Try to catch me if you can.

Teacher: (Make sure Jim and Sara do not try to catch them and just look confused.) The leprechauns continued to chant, "Try to catch me if you can," while they danced around Sara and Jim. Finally, Jim screamed, "Stop!"

Jim: Stop!

Teacher: And the leprechauns all stopped and faced Jim and Sara. The leprechauns looked very happy. Sara asked, "Who are you?"

Sara: Who are you?

Teacher: They proudly replied, "We're leprechauns. Why are you here?"

Leprechauns: We're leprechauns. Why are you here?

Teacher: Jim and Sara said, "We're looking for Gold."

Jim and Sara: We're looking for Gold.

Teacher: The leprechauns' eyes lit up. They became excited about finding Gold. They all said, "Gold!"

Leprechauns: Gold!

Teacher: The leprechauns asked, "Do you have a map?"

Leprechauns: Do you have a map?

Teacher: Jim said, "Well, yes we do."

Jim: Well, yes we do.

Teacher: The leprechauns bravely asked, "Can we see your map?"

Leprechauns: Can we see your map?

Teacher: Sara looked at the map and said, "I guess so. Here it is."

Sara: I guess so. Here it is. (She hands them the map.)

Teacher: The leprechauns grabbed it and got into a huddle to study the map. After a short time, one leprechaun stepped forward with the map and handed it back to Sara and Jim and said, "Thank you. You need to go that way (teacher points to the left) to find Gold."

Leprechaun: Thank you. You need to go that way (points to the left) to find Gold.

Teacher: Sara and Jim took back the map, and the leprechauns giggled as they went back into the forest (sit in the audience). They knew they were going to find the place where Gold was before Sara and Jim did. Jim asked, "What was that all about?"

Jim: What was that all about?

Teacher: Sara shrugged her shoulders and said, "I don't know."

Sara: I don't know.

Teacher: They continued to walk through the green forest. Meanwhile, Evil One was at (his or her) evil castle. (Sara and Jim sit in the audience, and Evil One and Sidekick take center stage. As they take the stage, the audience boos and hisses.) Evil One rubbed (his or her) hands together and said (his or her) most famous line, "I want Gold."

Evil One: I want Gold.

Teacher: Evil One threw (his or her) head back and laughed the evil laugh. (Evil One laughs.) Sidekick pointed to Evil One and said, "(He or she) wants gold."

Sidekick: (He or she) wants Gold.

Teacher: Evil One turned to Sidekick and demanded, "Get my crystal ball."

Evil One: Get my crystal ball.

Teacher: Sidekick picked up a pretend crystal ball and placed it in front of Evil One on a pretend table. Evil One waved (his or her) hands over the ball and said, "What's this I see?"

Evil One: What's this I see?

Teacher: "Two kids alone, looking for Gold?"

Evil One: Two kids alone, looking for Gold?

Teacher: Evil One shouted his famous line, "I want Gold!"

Evil One: I want Gold!

Teacher: Evil One threw (his or her) head back and laughed (his or her) evil laugh. (Evil One laughs.) Sidekick pointed to Evil One and said, "(He or she) wants gold."

Sidekick: (He or she) wants gold.

Teacher: Meanwhile, Sara and Jim were still walking through the green forest. (Evil One and Sidekick sit down in the audience.) They both stopped to look at the map. Suddenly, Evil One and Sidekick appeared and stood to their left. (Audience boos and hisses.) Evil One said, "I want Gold!"

Evil One: I want Gold!

Teacher: Then (he or she) threw (his or her) head back and laughed an evil laugh. (Evil One laughs.) Sidekick pointed to Evil One and said, "(He or she) wants Gold."

Sidekick: (He or she) wants Gold.

Teacher: Evil One then waved (his or her) hands toward the map and said the magic words. (If Evil One has not thought of magic words, tell the student some. For example, "Abracadabra, zap!") After Evil One said the magic words, Jim and Sara were shocked. Jim said, "What happened to our map?"

Jim: What happened to our map?

Teacher: Sara was so surprised, she said, "I don't know! It just went blank."

Sara: I don't know! It just went blank.

Teacher: Suddenly, Magic Wizard appeared. (Audience says, "Poof!")

Teacher: Magic Wizard knew what Evil One had done and said, "That's not fair, Evil One."

Magic Wizard: That's not fair, Evil One.

Teacher: Magic Wizard waved (his or her) hands toward the map and said the magic words. (Same as with the Evil One; if Magic Wizard does not have any magic words ready, supply some.) As Magic Wizard said these words, the map came back. Jim said, "Look, the map is appearing!"

Jim: Look, the map is appearing!

Teacher: Sara was so relieved, she said, "That was close."

Sara: That was close.

Teacher: Evil One looked upset and complained, "Drats, foiled again!"

Evil One: Drats, foiled again!

Teacher: Evil One added, "But I saw the map, and I will find Gold!"

Evil One: But I saw the map, and I will find Gold!

Teacher: And Evil One and Sidekick left. (Audience boos and hisses.) Magic Wizard warned Sara and Jim, "You must be very careful."

Magic Wizard: You must be very careful.

Teacher: Jim and Sara both said, "We will. Thank you, Magic Wizard."

Jim and Sara: We will. Thank you, Magic Wizard.

Teacher: And Magic Wizard disappeared. (Audience says, "Poof!") Sara and Jim continued on their journey to find Gold. Sara looked at the map and said, "We're almost to Pirate Bridge."

Sara: We're almost to Pirate Bridge.

Teacher: The pirates and the Parrot came onstage. They all looked mean and scary. Captain Pirate said, "Hey there, matey."

Captain: Hey there, matey.

Teacher: Parrot repeated with a squawk, "Hey there, matey."

Parrot: (Squawk) Hey there, matey.

Teacher: Sara and Jim turned around quickly to face the pirates. They were scared. Their knees were shaking; they began biting their nails. Jim stuttered, "P-p-p-lease don't hurt us."

Jim: P-p-p-lease don't hurt us.

Teacher: Captain asked in a loud, booming voice, "Why are you here?"

Captain: Why are you here?

Teacher: Parrot repeated, "(Squawk) Why are you here?"

Parrot: (Squawk) Why are you here?

Teacher: Sara replied, "We're looking f-f-for Gold."

Sara: We're looking f-f-for Gold.

Teacher: All of the pirates' eyes widened. They were excited about finding Gold for themselves. They all said, "Gold?"

All Pirates: Gold?

Teacher: Parrot repeated, "(Squawk) Gold?"

Parrot: (Squawk) Gold?

Teacher: Captain said in a sweet and calm voice, "Let me see your map."

Captain: Let me see your map.

Teacher: Sara's hands were shaking as she handed Captain the map. He snatched it away from her. The pirates got into a huddle and all looked at the map. After a short time, Captain handed the map back to Sara and Jim. Captain said, "Here's your map. You may cross Pirate Bridge."

Captain: Here's your map. You may cross Pirate Bridge.

Teacher: Captain also let them know, "We will find Gold before you."

Captain: We will find Gold before you.

Teacher: Parrot repeated, "(Squawk) We will find Gold before you."

Parrot: (Squawk) We will find Gold before you.

Teacher: And the pirates laughed as they left. Sara and Jim were glad when they were gone. Jim said, "What was that all about?"

Jim: What was that all about?

Teacher: Sara said, "I don't know."

Sara: I don't know.

Scene change: Have Sara and Jim stand on the opposite side of the stage from Gold. The leprechauns sit in a circle on the far left, Evil One and Sidekick sit in the center, and the pirates sit in a circle far right. They are all pretending to dig for Gold, sitting down. Tell them to pretend to talk but not to make any noise. After everyone is in place, the play can continue.

From *Little Plays for Little People.* © 1996. Teacher Ideas Press. (800) 237-6124.

Teacher: Sara and Jim looked at the map. Jim said, "This is the place."

Jim: This is the place.

Teacher: Sara looked at all of the people there. She asked, "Why are so many people here?"

Sara: Why are so many people here?

Teacher: Jim shrugged his shoulders and said, "I don't know."

Jim: I don't know.

Teacher: Sara pointed across the stage and said, "Look, Gold!"

Sara: Look, Gold!

Teacher: Everyone looked up and said, "Where?"

All: Where?

Teacher: Gold walked behind everyone who was digging and met Sara and Jim in the middle of the stage. Sara and Jim gave Gold a big hug. Sara said, "Gold, we were worried about you."

Sara: Gold, we were worried about you.

Teacher: Gold asked, "How did you find me?"

Gold: How did you find me?

Teacher: Jim said, "We had a map."

Jim: We had a map.

Teacher: The leprechauns stood up and looked very angry and said, "We thought we would be rich."

Leprechauns: We thought we would be rich.

Teacher: The leprechauns stormed into the audience and sat down. The pirates stood up and said, "Gold is a person?!"

Pirates: Gold is a person?!

Teacher: They stormed into the audience and sat down. Evil One and Sidekick stood up. Evil One said, "Drats, foiled once again!"

Evil One: Drats, foiled once again!

Teacher: And they stormed into the audience and sat down. Gold asked Sara and Jim, "What was that all about?"

Gold: What was that all about?

Teacher: Sara said, "I don't know."

Sara: I don't know.

Teacher: Jim said, "All we said was that we were looking for Gold."

Jim: All we said was that we were looking for Gold.

Teacher: Gold said with a smile, "And here I am."

Gold: And here I am.

The End

8
Magic Carrot

Play Synopsis

Magic Carrot is the story of a young girl, Susie, who does not like Christmas because she never gets the presents she wants. A Magic Bunny appears to take her on a journey to the North Pole. The Magic Bunny does the wrong spell twice, and they end up in the land of Halloween and then the land of Independence Day. Finally, the Magic Bunny gets the spell right and gets them to the North Pole, where they meet Santa Claus and the elves. Susie helps one of the elves make presents instead of picking her own. It is there she discovers the true meaning of the holidays—giving.

Character Descriptions

Cast size: The cast size can range from 10 to 30 students. For classes of fewer than 10 students, those who play the ghosts can also play the firecracker wizards and elves. For larger classes, I suggest having not more than five ghosts, five firecracker wizards, and five elves. If your class is bigger, increase the number of any of those three parts to accommodate your class size.

Susie wants all the presents in the world. She starts out selfish and demanding. By the end of the journey, she understands the value in giving.

Magic Bunny has a good heart but is not the greatest Magic Bunny. Because the character is always mixing up the spells, the Bunny and Susie end up in the wrong places. Magic Bunny also hates being mistaken for the Easter Bunny.

Halloween King is scary and mysterious, best played by the student who understands how to change voice and body for the character.

Goblin runs across the stage and takes the magic carrot. This part is short but should be played by a student who can change voice and body to act like a goblin.

Queen of Independence Day is proper and correct. She stands straight and tall and is best played by the natural-actress type of student.

Santa Claus is jolly and bright. He is a happy man and quite wise, best played by an outgoing student.

Big Elf does not necessarily have to be big. This elf has trouble making toys and is sad. This part can be played by any type of student.

Elves love to build toys and help Santa. There should be a minimum of two elves.

Ghosts are scary and laugh scary laughs. There should be a minimum of two ghosts.

Firecracker wizards make and test the firecrackers. There should be a minimum of two firecracker wizards.

Characters to Use for Auditions

Halloween King says, "I am the Halloween King."

Queen of Independence Day says, "I am the Queen."

Magic Bunny says, "I am not the Easter Bunny! I'm a Magic Bunny."

Susie says, "I want my presents."

Santa Claus says, "Ho, ho, ho."

For each character, look for students who can change their voices or stances or both for the audition. For example, encourage students who audition to be Santa Claus to pretend to have a big belly. Use the audition worksheet on the next page to make any notes or comments.

Susie

Magic Bunny

Halloween King

Goblin

Queen of Independence Day

Santa Claus

Big Elf

Elves (at least two)

Ghosts (at least two)

Firecracker wizards (at least two)

Notes and comments:

Final Cast List

Susie

Magic Bunny

Halloween King

Goblin

Queen of Independence Day

Santa Claus

Big Elf

Elves

Ghosts

Firecracker wizards

Notes and comments:

Once the play is cast, explain to the Goblin that after he takes the magic carrot he must give it to the Halloween King in the audience. Have students who have the same parts sit together (e.g., ghosts sit with ghosts, etc.)

Sound Effects

Before beginning the play, practice the following sound effects with the audience:

> When the Magic Bunny first appears, the audience says, "Poof!"
>
> Whenever the Magic Bunny is called the Easter Bunny, the audience groans.
>
> The audience says, "One, two, three" at the end of each spell, along with the Magic Bunny.
>
> Firecrackers (audience makes explosion sounds like firecrackers going off).

Technical Aspects

There is no set for this play. I suggest providing a carrot prop for the Magic Bunny.

Suggestions

This is a great play to do around the holidays. There are endless options for costumes. Santa can wear a Santa suit. Magic Bunny can have bunny ears and a tail. If you perform this play for parents, I suggest making costumes with your class.

Magic Carrot: The Play

Teacher: There was a little girl named Susie who sat alone in her room. She did not like Christmas because she never got any of the toys that she wanted. She whined all the time, "I wish I could have all the presents I want!"

Susie: I wish I could have all the presents I want!

Teacher: One day, while she was pouting in her room, a talking bunny appeared. (Audience says, "Poof!") Susie was so surprised, she asked, "Are you the Easter Bunny?"

Susie: Are you the Easter Bunny? (Audience groans.)

Teacher: The bunny rolled (his or her) eyes and said, "No, I'm not the Easter Bunny."

Magic Bunny: No, I'm not the Easter Bunny.

Teacher: The bunny looked quite upset and said, "I'm tired of people thinking I'm the Easter Bunny. I'm a Magic Bunny."

Magic Bunny: I'm tired of people thinking I'm the Easter Bunny. I'm a Magic Bunny.

Teacher: Susie could hardly believe there was a Magic Bunny in her room. She asked, "Why are you here, Magic Bunny?"

Susie: Why are you here, Magic Bunny?

Teacher: The Magic Bunny wiggled (his or her) nose and replied, "I'm here to grant your wish."

Magic Bunny: I'm here to grant your wish.

Teacher: Susie looked confused. She did not understand what the Magic Bunny meant. So the Magic Bunny explained, "You wished for all the presents you want."

Magic Bunny: You wished for all the presents you want.

Teacher: Susie got very excited and started to jump up and down and say all the things she wanted. "I want a doll house, and a little car for kids, and—"

Susie: I want a doll house, and a little car for kids, and—

Teacher: The Magic Bunny shook (his or her) head no. Susie noticed and got mad and said, "I thought you said you were here to grant my wish!"

Susie: I thought you said you were here to grant my wish!

Teacher: The Magic Bunny nodded (his or her) head yes and said, "Yes, I am, but you must ask Santa Claus yourself."

Magic Bunny: Yes, I am, but you must ask Santa Claus yourself. (Audience says, "Ho, ho, ho.")

Teacher: Susie was so excited, she said, "I get to meet Santa Claus?"

Susie: I get to meet Santa Claus? (Audience says, "Ho, ho, ho.")

Teacher: The Magic Bunny replied, "I will take you to the North Pole."

Magic Bunny: I will take you to the North Pole.

Teacher: The Magic Bunny waved (his or her) magic carrot and said, "Hum did dee dum, hum did dee dee."

Magic Bunny: Hum did dee dum, hum did dee dee.

Teacher: The Bunny continued, "Take us to the land of gifts in the night."

Magic Bunny: Take us to the land of gifts in the night.

Everyone: One, two, three.

Teacher: And the Magic Bunny waved the magic carrot. Suddenly, some ghosts came running across the stage and circled the Magic Bunny and Susie. Susie stuttered, "I d-d-don't think that you h-h-have the right l-l-land."

Susie: I d-d-don't think that you h-h-have the right l-l-land.

Teacher: The Magic Bunny looked worried and said, "Me neither."

Magic Bunny: Me neither.

Teacher: The ghosts circled them and laughed scary laughs. They all chanted, "Welcome to the land of Halloween."

Ghosts: Welcome to the land of Halloween.

Teacher: They laughed and laughed. One goblin came running across the stage and took the magic carrot. Magic Bunny cried, "Oh no, my magic carrot!"

Magic Bunny: Oh no, my magic carrot!

Teacher: The ghosts went howling back down into the audience. Susie said, "This place is creepy. Get us out of here."

Susie: This place is creepy. Get us out of here.

Teacher: The Magic Bunny shrugged (his or her) shoulders and said, "I guess I was wrong. The land of gifts in the night is Halloween land."

Magic Bunny: I guess I was wrong. The land of gifts in the night is Halloween land.

Teacher: Susie and the Magic Bunny did not know what to do. The Magic Bunny said, "We can't leave unless we get back the magic carrot."

Magic Bunny: We can't leave unless we get back the magic carrot.

Teacher: Suddenly, there was a loud noise (everyone claps once) and a creature appeared. "I am the Halloween King," he said in a loud voice.

Halloween King: I am the Halloween King.

Teacher: He looked closely at Susie and the Magic Bunny. "Why are you here, Easter Bunny and friend?" he demanded.

Halloween King: Why are you here, Easter Bunny and friend? (Audience groans.)

Teacher: The Magic Bunny cleared (his or her) throat and boldly said, "I am not the Easter Bunny, I am a Magic Bunny. We are here by mistake. Please give us the magic carrot and we will be on our way."

Magic Bunny: I am not the Easter Bunny, I am a Magic Bunny. We are here by mistake. Please give us the magic carrot and we will be on our way.

Teacher: The Halloween King looked at them longer and said, "Halloween means to give the gift of fright to people."

Halloween King: Halloween means to give the gift of fright to people.

Teacher: Then Susie thought of an idea for getting back the magic carrot. She would pretend that it scared her, so the Halloween King would want to return it. She said, "That magic carrot is dangerous. It scares me."

Susie: That magic carrot is dangerous. It scares me.

Teacher: The Magic Bunny stared at Susie and said, "What are you talking about? It's just a carrot!"

Magic Bunny: What are you talking about? It's just a carrot!

Teacher: Susie glared at the Magic Bunny. She whispered, "This is our chance to get back the magic carrot."

Susie: This is our chance to get back the magic carrot.

Teacher: The Magic Bunny understood and added, "Oh yes, I'm very scared of that carrot."

Magic Bunny: Oh yes, I'm very scared of that carrot.

Teacher: The Halloween King smiled a scary smile and said, "Scared, really? I can't think of a better gift of fright."

Halloween King: Scared, really? I can't think of a better gift of fright.

Teacher: The Halloween King handed the magic carrot to them. Susie and the Magic Bunny shrieked in fear. The Halloween King went back to his land of gifts in the night. The Magic Bunny said, "Well, let's get out of here!

Magic Bunny: Well, let's get out of here!

Teacher: Susie said, "Please get it right this time!

Susie: Please get it right this time!

Teacher: So the Magic Bunny began the spell, "Hum did dee dum, hum did dee dee."

Magic Bunny: Hum did dee dum, hum did dee dee.

Teacher: The Magic Bunny continued, "Take us to the land of lights."

Magic Bunny: Take us to the land of lights.

Everyone: One, two, three.

Teacher: The Magic Bunny waved the magic carrot and wiggled (his or her) nose. They both looked around. It didn't look like the North Pole. Suddenly, there were loud explosions (firecrackers). They both covered their ears. Susie said, "What's that noise?"

Susie: What's that noise?

Teacher: The Magic Bunny couldn't hear Susie. Some people came running onstage and circled them. They chanted, "We are the firecracker wizards. We're free!" The firecracker wizards threw their hands in the air and pointed to the sky. The sky was all lit up. "Oh, no," said the Magic Bunny, "the land of lights is the land of Independence Day!"

Magic Bunny: Oh no, the land of lights is the land of Independence Day!

Teacher: Susie said, "You messed up the spell again!"

Susie: You messed up the spell again!

Teacher: Before the Magic Bunny could answer, a firecracker wizard approached them and said, "Is that a firecracker?"

Firecracker Wizard: Is that a firecracker?

Teacher: And in a flash, Firecracker Wizard grabbed the magic carrot and took it to be tested. Any firecrackers that did not work would be shredded. The Magic Bunny said, "Not again!"

Magic Bunny: Not again!

Teacher: Just then, a woman came forward. She introduced herself. "I am the Queen of Independence Day."

Queen: I am the Queen of Independence Day.

Teacher: She continued, "You are in the land of Fourth of July, where we give the gift of freedom."

Queen: You are in the land of Fourth of July, where we give the gift of freedom.

Teacher: She looked closely at the two and said, "Why are you here, Easter Bunny? And who is your friend?"

Queen: Why are you here, Easter Bunny? (Audience groans.) And who is your friend?

Teacher: The Magic Bunny got upset and said, "I am not the Easter Bunny, and this is Susie."

Magic Bunny: I am not the Easter Bunny, and this is Susie.

Teacher: Susie told the Queen of Independence Day, "That Firecracker Wizard took our key to freedom."

Susie: That Firecracker Wizard took our key to freedom.

Teacher: The Queen looked displeased. She demanded, "What was it that was taken?"

Queen: What was it that was taken?

Teacher: The Magic Bunny said, "A magic carrot."

Magic Bunny: A magic carrot.

Teacher: The Queen snapped her fingers (everybody snaps). Firecracker Wizard came out with the magic carrot and handed it to the Queen. She handed it to the Magic Bunny and said, "Here is your gift of freedom."

Queen: Here is your gift of freedom.

Teacher: Magic Bunny took the magic carrot and said, "Thank you."

Magic Bunny: Thank you.

Teacher: The Queen of Independence Day left the two alone. Susie said, "Now, can we get to my presents?"

Susie: Now, can we get to my presents?

Teacher: Magic Bunny said, "Of course, be patient."

Magic Bunny: Of course, be patient.

Teacher: Magic Bunny began the spell, "Hum did dee dum, hum did dee dee."

Magic Bunny: Hum did dee dum, hum did dee dee.

Teacher: Magic Bunny continued, "Take us to the land of Santa Claus."

Magic Bunny: Take us to the land of Santa Claus.

Everyone: One, two, three.

Teacher: Magic Bunny waved the magic carrot and wiggled (his or her) nose. They both looked around. Susie said, "I hope you got it right this time."

Susie: I hope you got it right this time.

Teacher: Suddenly, little elves came rushing in and chanted, "Welcome to Christmas Land!"

Elves: Welcome to Christmas Land!

Teacher: Susie beamed with happiness and said, "Finally, my presents!"

Susie: Finally, my presents!

Teacher: The elves stood in a circle and quietly worked on toys. Santa Claus entered with a big "Ho, ho, ho."

Santa: Ho, ho, ho.

Teacher: He came over to Susie and the Magic Bunny and asked, "How are you, Magic Bunny?"

Santa: How are you, Magic Bunny?

Teacher: Magic Bunny said, "Fine. I'm glad you did not think I was the Easter Bunny!"

Magic Bunny: Fine. I'm glad you did not think I was the Easter Bunny!

Teacher: Santa looked at Susie and said, "And who is this?"

Santa: And who is this?

Teacher: Susie came forward and said, "I'm Susie, and this is the land of getting my presents."

Susie: I'm Susie, and this is the land of getting my presents.

Teacher: Santa laughed and said, "OK. You have 10 minutes to choose your presents."

Santa: OK. You have 10 minutes to choose your presents.

Teacher: Susie was so excited. Santa left with a "Ho, ho, ho."

Santa: Ho, ho, ho.

Teacher: And the Magic Bunny followed him. Susie did not know where to start. She watched the elves working, then Big Elf stormed away and sat down. (He or she) began to cry. Susie said, "What's wrong?"

Susie: What's wrong?

Teacher: Big Elf cried and cried. Finally, (he or she) said, "I can't make toys. My hands are too big!"

Big Elf: I can't make toys. My hands are too big!

Teacher: Susie looked at the elf. She looked around the room. She said, "I can help you if you like."

Susie: I can help you if you like.

Teacher: Big Elf looked at her in surprise. He said, "Yes, I would like that."

Big Elf: Yes, I would like that.

Teacher: So, Susie helped Big Elf build a toy. (They pretend to build.) Santa Claus and the Magic Bunny came back into the room. Santa said, "Your time is up."

Santa: Your time is up.

Teacher: Magic Bunny said, "Where are all your presents?"

Magic Bunny: Where are all your presents?

Teacher: Susie said, "Oh, I helped this elf make a toy instead."

Susie: Oh, I helped this elf make a toy instead.

Teacher: Santa said, "I thought Christmas was about presents to you."

Santa: I thought Christmas was about presents to you.

Teacher: Susie thought for a moment and said, "I guess not. It's about giving, isn't it?"

Susie: I guess not. It's about giving, isn't it?

Teacher: Magic Bunny and Santa looked very happy. Magic Bunny said, "Yes, it's about giving, which is what you did for Big Elf."

Magic Bunny: Yes, it's about giving, which is what you did for Big Elf.

Teacher: And Susie learned the true value is not in getting all the presents she wants. It's in giving to others.

The End

9
The Little Ghost

Play Synopsis

The Little Ghost is a great Halloween play about goblins, mummies, witches, ghosts, and monsters. The Little Ghost cannot fly and decides to go into the forest to try to be someone else. During the journey, the Little Ghost discovers how to fly and regains self-confidence. In the end, the Little Ghost finds that it is best to be just who you are—in this case, a ghost.

Character Descriptions

Cast size: The ideal cast size for this play is 15 students. If you have fewer than that, have the same students play the parts of goblins, ghosts, witches, and mummies. If you have more than that, increase the number of goblins, ghosts, witches, and mummies to suit your class size.

Little Ghost is very young and does not understand what it means to really try. Rather than working at flying, the ghost decides it would be easier to try to be something else. The Little Ghost is best played by a student who is expressive.

Captain Ghost is the leader of all the ghosts. This character is wise and all knowing. Captain Ghost sends the Little Ghost away, knowing what will happen. This role is best played by a student with a strong stage presence.

Rock/Frog begins as a rock. The Little Ghost does a spell and turns the rock into a frog, who hops away. This part should be played by a student who can come on stage alone without hesitation. Although it is a smaller part, it is an important one.

Monster is a caring creature who teaches the Little Ghost an invaluable lesson—not to give up. Monster is also friendly and likes to help.

Ghosts love to fly and make noise. They are not very nice to the Little Ghost. There should be at least two ghosts.

Mummies should be played by students who can walk stiffly and keep their faces sullen. There should be at least three mummies.

Goblins are curious creatures. They are hunched over and their faces are scrunched up. They try to be scary, but they are really nice. The way they growl and hunch over makes them seem scarier than they really are. There should be at least three goblins.

Witches love to make spells. They love to cackle and ride their brooms. They are also mysterious and are not fond of intruders. Witches no. 1 and 2 have some lines in the play and should be assigned to the stronger students. There should be at least two witches in addition to Witches no. 1 and 2.

Characters to Use for Auditions

Because there are so many different creatures of the night in this play, it is important that they not just say their lines but also change their bodies like their characters' bodies. Before auditions, show students how the different characters stand. Use the following descriptions:

A ghost stands like this: arms out, ready to fly.

A goblin stands like this: hunched over and face scrunched up.

A mummy stands like this: arms out and walking stiffly in place.

A witch stands like this: mean face and body slightly hunched over.

After showing students, have them all stand in place and act out the four parts. This mass audition gives you the opportunity to observe which students are best for which parts. Begin the individual auditions after students have all had a chance to act out the four parts. Use the following lines:

Ghost says, "I am a ghost, oooohhh."

Goblin says, "I am a goblin, (growl)."

Mummy says, "I am a mummy, aaahhhhh."

Witch says, "I am a witch, (cackle)."

Audition Worksheet

Little Ghost

Captain Ghost

Monster

Rock/Frog

Witch no. 1

Witch no. 2

Witches (at least two in addition to witches 1 and 2)

Ghosts (at least two)

Goblins (at least three)

Mummies (at least three)

Notes and comments:

Little Ghost

Captain Ghost

Monster

Rock/Frog

Witch no. 1

Witch no. 2

Witches

Ghosts

Goblins

Mummies

Notes and comments:

Sound Effects

The sound effects include the following:

> Audience members stamp their feet to make the footsteps sound.

> Audience says, "Poof!" when the rock becomes a frog.

> Goblins growl.

> Mummies groan, "Aaahhhh."

> Wind blows.

> Witches cackle.

Technical Aspects

There is no set for this play. If this is a full performance, costumes for all of the characters would be great. Making costumes could be an art project for students.

Suggestions

This play is great to do for Halloween. Students love being creepy and scary characters, and *The Little Ghost* provides them the opportunity to do so. This play also ties in with the theme of not giving up, even if something seems difficult. Follow-up discussions may be useful, allowing students to talk about times that they gave up or did not give up on something and what happened.

The Little Ghost: The Play

Teacher: Once upon a time there was a land of lots of scary creatures. There were ghosts, witches, goblins, and things that went bump in the night. And one scary night, the ghosts came running in circles, and they said, "Oooohhh."

Ghosts: Oooohhh.

Teacher: And there was the Captain Ghost, who bellowed to all, "Ghosts be scary, ghosts give fright, on this cold night!"

Captain Ghost: Ghosts be scary, ghosts give fright, on this cold night!

Teacher: And all of the ghosts looked and moved like very frightening creatures. They would fly around. (Ghosts pretend, with their arms out, that they can fly.) And then one Little Ghost joined them and did not sound very scary. The Little Ghost watched the other ghosts fly. The Little Ghost tried to fly but could not. The other ghosts said, "What's wrong with you?"

Ghosts: What's wrong with you?

Teacher: And the Little Ghost replied, "I don't know."

Little Ghost: I don't know.

Teacher: The Little Ghost looked very sad. All the other ghosts went back to being scary and looking scary and flying. The Little Ghost found (he or she) did not like being a ghost. Little Ghost said, "I'm not a good ghost. I can't fly."

Little Ghost: I'm not a good ghost. I can't fly.

Teacher: The Captain Ghost came over to the Little Ghost. The other ghosts went off into the night, scaring people. (Ghosts go into the audience.) The Captain Ghost said, "You do not look happy."

Captain Ghost: You do not look happy.

Teacher: The Little Ghost replied, "I'm not happy here, and I can't fly."

98

From *Little Plays for Little People.* © 1996. Teacher Ideas Press. (800) 237-6124.

Little Ghost: I'm not happy here, and I can't fly.

Teacher: The Captain Ghost sighed heavily. (You do this and the Captain will imitate you.) Then the Captain said, "You are a young ghost. You will learn."

Captain Ghost: You are a young ghost. You will learn.

Teacher: The Little Ghost still looked unhappy and said, "I don't like being a ghost. I want to be something else."

Little Ghost: I don't like being a ghost. I want to be something else.

Teacher: The Captain looked at the Little Ghost. There was a silence. Finally, the Captain said, "Then try to be something else. There are plenty of creatures to be."

Captain Ghost: Then try to be something else. There are plenty of creatures to be.

Teacher: The Little Ghost was happy that the Captain gave permission to be something else. The Captain Ghost said, "But remember, you cannot change who you are."

Captain Ghost: But remember, you cannot change who you are.

Teacher: The Little Ghost nodded and said, "OK."

Little Ghost: OK.

Teacher: The Little Ghost did not really understand what that meant. But (he or she) decided to explore the forest and find something else to be. The Little Ghost walked and walked and walked. A wind began to blow (audience makes wind sound), and it kept getting louder and louder. Suddenly, the Little Ghost could hear lots of footsteps coming toward (him or her). (Audience makes footsteps sound.) Mummies walked up to the Little Ghost and asked, "Who are you?"

Mummies: Who are you?

Teacher: And the Little Ghost stuttered, "I'm j-j-just a little, um, well, who are you?"

Little Ghost: I'm j-j-just a little, um, well, who are you?

Teacher: The Little Ghost did not want to tell them (he or she) was a ghost. The mummies looked closely at the ghost and said, "We're mummies."

Mummies: We're mummies.

Teacher: The Little Ghost said, "What do mummies do?"

Little Ghost: What do mummies do?

Teacher: The mummies all put their arms out and walked stiffly around the Little Ghost. They all groaned, "Ahhhhhhh."

Mummies: Ahhhhhh.

Teacher: The Little Ghost thought that the mummies were pretty cool. (He or she) wanted to know how to become one. The Little Ghost said, "I want to be a mummy."

Little Ghost: I want to be a mummy.

Teacher: The mummies said, "To be a mummy, you first have to learn how to walk like a mummy."

Mummies: To be a mummy, you first have to learn how to walk like a mummy.

Teacher: The mummies all put out their arms. The Little Ghost put out (his or her) arms. The mummies all made scary faces. The Little Ghost made a scary face. The mummies all walked stiffly (in place). The Little Ghost walked stiffly (in place). The mummies said, "That's right."

Mummies: That's right.

Teacher: The Little Ghost said, "I like being a mummy. This is fun."

Little Ghost: I like being a mummy. This is fun.

Teacher: The mummies said, "Now you have to groan like a mummy, ahhhhh."

Mummies: Now you have to groan like a mummy, ahhhhh.

Teacher: The Little Ghost said, "That's easy, oooohhhhhh."

Little Ghost: That's easy, oooohhhhhhhhh.

Teacher: The mummies said, "Oh no, that's not right."

Mummies: Oh no, that's not right.

Teacher: The Little Ghost could only make noises like a ghost. The mummies said, "We're sorry. You can't be a mummy."

Mummies: We're sorry. You can't be a mummy.

Teacher: The mummies started to walked stiffly with their arms out into the night (back to the audience). The Little Ghost pleaded, "But wait. I can do it. Wait."

Little Ghost: But wait. I can do it. Wait.

Teacher: But it was no use, the mummies were gone. The Little Ghost looked sad again. (He or she) began wandering through the forest again. The wind blew through the forest (audience makes wind sound). The Little Ghost said, "I'll never be anything but a ghost."

Little Ghost: I'll never be anything but a ghost.

Teacher: Just then, there was some growling. The Little Ghost looked around. Suddenly, some goblins came leaping out and circled the Little Ghost. "We are goblins. Who are you?" they growled.

Goblins: We are goblins. Who are you?

Teacher: The Little Ghost looked at the goblins. They were interesting creatures. Their faces were all scrunched up, and they could not stand straight. They were all hunched over with their arms dangling at their sides. The Little Ghost said, "I'm a ghost, but I would like to be a goblin."

Little Ghost: I'm a ghost, but I would like to be a goblin.

Teacher: The goblins growled in delight. They said, "To be a goblin, you have to hunch over like us."

Goblins: To be a goblin, you have to hunch over like us.

Teacher: The Little Ghost hunched over as they were. The goblins said, "Good, now your face like this." And they all scrunched up their faces.

Goblins: Good, now your face like this.

Teacher: The Little Ghost scrunched up (his or her) face. The goblins said, "Just one more thing—growl."

Goblins: Just one more thing—growl.

Teacher: And all the goblins growled mean and frightening growls. The Little Ghost opened (his or her) mouth and went, "Oooohhhh."

Little Ghost: Oooohhhh.

Teacher: The goblins said, "That's not a growl."

Goblins: That's not a growl.

Teacher: The Little Ghost looked so disappointed. The goblins began to leave. "Wait!" cried the Little Ghost.

Little Ghost: Wait!

Teacher: But the goblins left. The Little Ghost was left all alone again. The Little Ghost said, "I'll never be anything but a ghost who can't fly."

Little Ghost: I'll never be anything but a ghost who can't fly.

Teacher: And the Little Ghost continued through the night. The Little Ghost came to a cave. It was an old and smelly cave. (He or she) walked inside and found a bunch of people circled around a huge pot. (Witches onstage in a circle.) They were all stirring something in the pot. The Little Ghost quietly came in—any ghost can move quietly—and watched. The witches cackled as they stirred. (Witches cackle. You show them how first.) They began pouring things into the pot. One witch said, "Pour it in slowly."

Witch no. 1: Pour it in slowly.

Teacher: They all chanted the words, "Ala, ala, zam, ala, ala, zoom."

Witches: Ala, ala, zam, ala, ala, zoom.

Teacher: They continued, "We're making potions, 'cause we love to."

Witches: We're making potions, 'cause we love to.

Teacher: And the witches waved their hands over the bubbling pot. One witch said, "I'll get the magic wands."

Witch no. 2: I'll get the magic wands.

Teacher: And the witch got the wands and brought them to the others. When they all had them, they waved those over the pot. The Little Ghost thought what they were doing was fascinating. The Little Ghost said, "Wow, they're witches."

Little Ghost: Wow, they're witches.

Teacher: The witches said, "What was that?"

Witches: What was that?

Teacher: And the Little Ghost timidly came out and said, "It was me."

Little Ghost: It was me.

Teacher: The witches came over and circled the Little Ghost. They said, "Who are you?"

Witches: Who are you?

Teacher: The Little Ghost said, "I'm a ghost, but I'd like to be a witch."

Little Ghost: I'm a ghost, but I'd like to be a witch.

Teacher: The witches all cackled again. One witch said, "Why?"

Witch no. 1: Why?

Teacher: The Little Ghost said, "Because the spells you do are neat. I want to learn how."

Little Ghost: Because the spells you do are neat. I want to learn how.

Teacher: The witches all looked at each other, amazed. They couldn't believe a ghost would want to be a witch. Ghosts can fly without a broomstick. But the witches decided to give the Little Ghost a chance. They said, "To be a witch, you have to be able to do spells."

Witches: To be a witch, you have to be able to do spells.

Teacher: The Little Ghost said, "OK."

Little Ghost: OK.

Teacher: One witch said, "Turn that rock (Rock/Frog comes onstage) into a frog."

Witch no. 2: Turn that rock into a frog.

Teacher: The Little Ghost went over to the rock and said, "Spells of spells."

Little Ghost: Spells of spells.

Teacher: The Little Ghost paused to think and said, "Make this hard rock catch flies."

Little Ghost: Make this hard rock catch flies.

Teacher: The Little Ghost knew spells that worked had to rhyme, so (he or she) said, "Turn it into a frog, right before our eyes."

Little Ghost: Turn it into a frog, right before our eyes.

Teacher: The Little Ghost said, "Zap!"

Little Ghost: Zap!

Teacher: And there was a poof (audience says, "Poof!"), and the rock began to ribbit. It was a frog. The frog hopped away (into the audience). The witches all clapped. They were very impressed. They said, "To be a witch, you also have to fly on a broom."

Witches: To be a witch, you also have to fly on a broom.

Teacher: All the witches went and got their brooms. They got on them, and Witch no. 1 handed one to the Little Ghost. They began to fly, and the Little Ghost followed them. (They all fly in place, steering their brooms.) The witches said, "That is very good."

Witches: That is very good.

Teacher: And they all landed back on the ground. They all put the brooms away. The witches then said, "Just one more thing."

Witches: Just one more thing.

Teacher: The Little Ghost nodded (his or her) head and was ready for what was last. The witches said, "To be a witch, you must be able to cackle."

Witches: To be a witch, you must be able to cackle.

Teacher: And all the witches began to cackle. They cackled and cackled. Then they said, "Now you try."

Witches: Now you try.

Teacher: The Little Ghost opened (his or her) mouth and tried to cackle, but all that came out was, "Ooooohhhh."

Little Ghost: Ooooohhhh.

Teacher: The witches looked horrified. They said, "That wasn't a cackle."

Witches: That wasn't a cackle.

Teacher: The witches looked at each other in disbelief. They all said, "You can't be a witch. You must leave."

Witches: You can't be a witch. You must leave.

Teacher: The Little Ghost protested and said, "I can do it. Please let me stay."

Little Ghost: I can do it. Please let me stay.

Teacher: The witches went back to working on their potions at the pot. They stood in a circle around the pot. The Little Ghost watched them and sadly walked away. (As the Little Ghost walks away, the witches sit in the audience.) Once again, the Little Ghost was all alone. The Little Ghost said, "If only I could fly, I would be a good ghost."

Little Ghost: If only I could fly, I would be a good ghost.

Teacher: The Little Ghost continued walking through the night. A little later, a Monster came howling out of the bushes. The Monster said, "I'm a Monster. Who are you?"

Monster: I'm a Monster. Who are you?

Teacher: The Little Ghost replied, "I'm a Little Ghost that can't fly."

Little Ghost: I'm a Little Ghost that can't fly.

Teacher: The Monster said, "Really? I'm a Monster that's not very scary."

Monster: Really? I'm a Monster that's not very scary.

Teacher: The Little Ghost laughed, "A Monster that's not scary?"

Little Ghost: A Monster that's not scary?

Teacher: The Monster looked hurt and said, "Yes, but I'm going to keep trying, 'cause that's what I am, a Monster."

Monster: Yes, but I'm going to keep trying, 'cause that's what I am, a Monster.

Teacher: The Little Ghost thought about this. Maybe, the Little Ghost thought, I gave up too quickly. But first the Little Ghost decided to help the Monster. The Little Ghost said, "Try to do this."

Little Ghost: Try to do this.

Teacher: And the Little Ghost made the scariest face ever. The Monster did the same face. The Little Ghost jumped back in fright and said, "That looked scary to me."

Little Ghost: That looked scary to me.

Teacher: The Monster smiled and said, "Really?"

Monster: Really?

Teacher: The Little Ghost nodded. The Monster said, "Now you have to fly."

Monster: Now you have to fly.

Teacher: The Little Ghost jumped in the air, but nothing happened. Then the Little Ghost got really determined and decided this was it. The Little Ghost said, "This time I'm going to do it."

Little Ghost: This time I'm going to do it.

Teacher: And the Little Ghost flew. (His or her) arms were out, and (he or she) was flying all around the Monster. As the Little Ghost flew away, (he or she) said, "Thank you."

Little Ghost: Thank you.

Teacher: The Monster waved good-bye and said, "Anytime."

Monster: Anytime.

Teacher: And the Monster faded from sight (Monster sits in audience). The Little Ghost was so happy. (He or she) flew all the way home to the other ghosts. (Ghosts and captain on stage.) They were all there being scary. The Little Ghost landed right in front of the Captain Ghost. The Captain Ghost said, "You're back!"

Captain Ghost: You're back!

Teacher: The Little Ghost said, "I tried to be a mummy, but I couldn't groan."

Little Ghost: I tried to be a mummy, but I couldn't groan. (Everyone groans.)

Teacher: The Little Ghost said, "I tried to be a goblin, but I couldn't growl."

Little Ghost: I tried to be a goblin, but I couldn't growl. (Audience growls.)

Teacher: The Little Ghost said, "I tried to be a witch, but I couldn't cackle."

Little Ghost: I tried to be a witch, but I couldn't cackle. (Audience cackles.)

Teacher: The Little Ghost said, "And then I finally realized I was a ghost, and all I could really do was oooooohhhhh."

Little Ghost: And then I finally realized I was a ghost, and all I could really do was oooooohhhhh.

Teacher: The Captain shook (his or her) head and said, "You see, you could fly all along."

Captain: You see, you could fly all along.

Teacher: The Little Ghost said, "I just needed to believe that I could be the very best at being me."

Little Ghost: I just needed to believe that I could be the very best at being me.

Teacher: And all the ghosts said, "Ooooohhhhh," and flew together. The Little Ghost was happy just being a ghost.

The End

From *Little Plays for Little People*. © 1996. Teacher Ideas Press. (800) 237-6124.

10
Little Red Riding Hood Lost in Fairy-tale Land

Play Synopsis

Little Red Riding Hood accidentally travels through Fairy-tale Land. Along the way, she manages to change "The Three Little Pigs" and "Snow White." On her journey, she meets Gleek, the manager of Fairy-tale Land, who tries to get her back to her own story. Finally, she ends up in Unwritten Fairy-tale Land and meets Stars, who gets her back to her own fairy tale.

Character Descriptions

Cast size: The ideal cast size is 12 students. If you have more students than that, increase the number of fairy-tale fairies, birds, and deer. If you have fewer than that, have students play multiple roles of fairy-tale fairies, birds, and deer.

Little Red Riding Hood is an energetic child. It doesn't bother her much that she is lost in Fairy-tale Land, but she does seem to get into a lot of trouble on her journey. Best played by a strong actress.

Wolf, from "The Three Little Pigs," growls and tries to scare people. But really, Wolf cannot hurt anyone at all. When confronted, Wolf's true self shows as a nice wolf who is hungry.

Pig is a nervous wreck. It would never occur to Pig to stand up to the Wolf.

Gleek is the manager of Fairy-tale Land. This character tries to make sure that all of the fairy tales happen the way they are written. Unfortunately, Gleek is not very good at correcting what goes wrong. Gleek gets frustrated easily but continues to try to keep things in order.

Snow White is the storybook version of this character. She is sweet and kind to all.

Snow White's Stepmother is an evil person who wants badly to get rid of Snow White. In this story, she is disguised as an old woman.

Stars is from Unwritten Fairy-tale Land. Stars does not exist in any story but is a magical and mysterious character, best played by a student who can act wise and all-knowing.

Fairy-tale fairies are all assistants to Gleek. Each time they enter, they wiggle their noses and blink their eyes. There should be a minimum of two fairy-tale fairies.

Birds and deer are in the "Snow White" scene. They are all helpful to Little Red Riding Hood and hide her from the evil Stepmother. There should be a minimum of one bird and one deer.

Characters to Use for Auditions

Students will be familiar with most of the characters in this story. Use the following characters:

Gleek says, "You messed up all the fairy tales!"

Little Red Riding Hood says, "This is not my story."

Snow White's Stepmother (an old woman) says, "I'll get Snow White!"

Stars says, "This is the Unwritten Fairy-tale Land."

Use the audition worksheet on the next page to record the students best suited to each part.

Audition Worksheet

Little Red Riding Hood

Wolf

Pig

Gleek

Snow White

Stepmother

Stars

Fairy-tale fairies (at least two)

Birds and deer (at least one of each)

Notes or comments:

Final Cast List

Little Red Riding Hood

Wolf

Pig

Gleek

Snow White

Stepmother

Stars

Fairy-tale fairies

Birds and deer

Notes or comments:

Sound Effects

The sound effects in this play include the following:

audience doing a spell with Stars

audience stamping their feet every time Little Red Riding Hood changes fairy tales

birds chirping

Rehearse the foot stamping sound effect with students. Explain that this is the sound that happens when Little Red Riding Hood changes lands. They should only stamp their feet for two to three seconds. Practice until everyone can stop at the same time.

Also, at the end of the story, Stars does a spell alone. Then the spell is repeated, and the audience does the spell with Stars. Practice the following once or twice before doing the play: Everyone stamps their feet three times: One, two, three. Everyone claps twice: One, two. Everyone stands up, turns around, and sits down. Make it clear to students to be careful when turning around so that no one gets hurt.

Technical Aspects

No set is required to do this play. An apple might be a useful prop for Snow White's Stepmother to have. Costumes are optional and would be great if this is performed for parents or other classes.

Suggestions

This play is based on the classic fairy tales. It is a great supplement if you are reading any of the classic fairy tales. A follow-up activity might be discussing how the stories could be changed and what would happen as a result. What would happen if the Three Little Pigs were Three Little Bears? What would happen if Sleeping Beauty never fell asleep? This activity could really encourage your students' creative energy.

Little Red Riding Hood Lost in Fairy-tale Land: The Play

Teacher: Little Red Riding Hood was walking through the forest. She could hear the birds chirping. (Audience makes chirping noise.) She loved walking through the forest that led to Grandma's house. She said, "I can't wait to see Grandma."

Red Riding Hood: I can't wait to see Grandma.

Teacher: She continued to walk through the forest. She heard some rustling in the bushes. (Audience makes rustling noise.) A voice boomed from the bushes and said, "Little Red Riding Hood, are you going to Grandma's?"

Audience: Little Red Riding Hood, are you going to Grandma's?

Teacher: Little Red Riding Hood looked around to see where the voice was coming from. She decided to run. She ran and ran (in place) through the forest. She tripped on a fallen branch and fell to the ground. There was a loud noise as she fell. (Audience stamps their feet.) She said, "Ouch!"

Red Riding Hood: Ouch!

Teacher: She looked around and realized she wasn't in the forest anymore. She looked confused and did not understand where she was. She seemed to be inside a small house made out of straw! She could not believe her eyes. Somehow, she had ended up in another fairy tale. A little Pig came in from another room (Pig enters) and gasped, "Who are you?"

Pig: Who are you?

Teacher: Little Red Riding Hood said, "I am Little Red Riding Hood."

Red Riding Hood: I am Little Red Riding Hood.

Teacher: The Pig looked at her in disbelief. (He or she) asked, "How did you get here?"

114

Pig: How did you get here?

Teacher: Little Red Riding Hood shrugged her shoulders. She really did not know how she got there or why. The last thing she remembered was running through the forest. Suddenly, there was a loud booming voice at the door (Wolf comes onstage) that bellowed, "Open the door, or I'll huff and I'll puff and I'll blow the door in!"

Wolf: Open the door, or I'll huff and I'll puff and I'll blow the door in!

Teacher: Little Red Riding Hood and the Pig started shaking with fear. Little Red Riding Hood said, "We're not safe. This house is made out of straw."

Red Riding Hood: We're not safe. This house is made out of straw.

Teacher: The Pig looked around at the house. (He or she) panicked and asked, "What'll we do?"

Pig: What'll we do?

Teacher: While they were deciding what to do, the Wolf was looking hungrier and hungrier by the minute. Little Red Riding Hood said, "That Wolf can't push us around!"

Red Riding Hood: That Wolf can't push us around!

Teacher: Little Red Riding Hood opened the door and marched outside to confront the Wolf. She said, "You can't push us around!"

Red Riding Hood: You can't push us around!"

Teacher: The Wolf growled at her, but she did not back down. She just stood there while the Wolf growled. The Wolf finally asked, "Aren't you scared of me?"

Wolf: Aren't you scared of me?

Teacher: Little Red Riding Hood shook her head no. The Wolf looked hurt. The Pig came out to see what was going on and asked, "Does this mean you'll leave now?"

Pig: Does this mean you'll leave now?

Teacher: The Wolf said, "But I'm hungry!"

Wolf: But I'm hungry!

Teacher: Little Red Riding Hood suddenly had an idea. She said, "Come inside and we will fix you something to eat."

Red Riding Hood: Come inside and we will fix you something to eat.

Teacher: The Wolf agreed, and they went inside to have some hot cereal. They sat down (on the floor) and the Pig brought them all bowls. The Wolf seemed to like it a lot and finished the whole bowl. (He or she) asked, "More, please."

Wolf: More, please.

Teacher: The Pig brought more. As they were eating, there was a loud noise. (Audience stamps their feet.) The Wolf and Pig disappeared (back to audience). Little Red Riding Hood looked around to see what was happening. Some fairy-tale fairies came running onstage and surrounded Little Red Riding Hood. She asked, "Who are you?"

Red Riding Hood: Who are you?

Teacher: The fairies wiggled their noses and blinked their eyes and said, "We're fairy-tale fairies. You're messing up everything!"

Fairies: We're fairy-tale fairies. You're messing up everything!

Teacher: Little Red Riding Hood looked confused. Another person came onstage (Gleek), pointed (his or her) finger at Little Red Riding Hood, and said, "There you are!"

Gleek: There you are!

Teacher: Little Red Riding Hood asked, "What is going on?"

Red Riding Hood: What is going on?

Teacher: Gleek said, "I am Gleek, manager of Fairy-tale Land."

Gleek: I am Gleek, manager of Fairy-tale Land.

Teacher: Gleek continued, "You are in the wrong fairy tale and just messed up 'The Three Little Pigs.' "

Gleek: You are in the wrong fairy tale and just messed up "The Three Little Pigs."

Teacher: The fairy-tale fairies all whispered among themselves. Gleek looked upset at Little Red Riding Hood. She said, "Then get me to my fairy tale!"

Red Riding Hood: Then get me to my fairy tale!

Teacher: Gleek waved (his or her) hands and hummed loudly. Little Red Riding Hood prepared herself to be back in her own fairy tale. She was looking forward to seeing Grandma. As Gleek hummed, the fairy-tale fairies disappeared (back into audience). There was that same loud noise again. (Audience stamps their feet.) Gleek disappeared, and Little Red Riding Hood looked around. She seemed to be in a forest again. Some birds and deer came up to her. She asked, "Which way to Grandma's?"

Red Riding Hood: Which way to Grandma's?

Teacher: The birds and deer looked at her, confused. They did not know what she was talking about. An old woman (Stepmother) came in sight. Little Red Riding Hood hid behind the deer. The old woman said, "If Snow White eats this apple, she will die!"

Stepmother: If Snow White eats this apple, she will die!

Teacher: The old woman laughed an evil laugh. Little Red Riding Hood whispered to the animals, "I have to stop her!"

Red Riding Hood: I have to stop her!

Teacher: Little Red Riding Hood stayed hidden with the animals. Then Snow White walked by, humming a pretty tune (anything). The old woman stopped her and said, "Would you like a bite of this shiny apple?"

Stepmother: Would you like a bite of this shiny apple?

Teacher: Snow White said, "Why, thank you, I would."

Snow White: Why, thank you, I would.

Teacher: And as Snow White was about to take the apple, Little Red Riding Hood jumped out and said, "Stop!"

Red Riding Hood: Stop!

Teacher: The old woman was so surprised she dropped the apple and ran away (into the audience). Little Red Riding Hood said, "She was trying to poison you!"

Red Riding Hood: She was trying to poison you!

Teacher: Snow White looked so surprised. She could not believe what she was hearing. She said, "Trying to poison me?"

Snow White: Trying to poison me?

Teacher: Before Little Red Riding Hood could answer, there was that loud noise again. (Audience stamps their feet.) The birds, deer, and Snow White disappeared (back to the audience). The fairy-tale fairies and Gleek appeared. The fairy-tale fairies wiggled their noses and blinked their eyes. They said, "You did it again!"

Fairies: You did it again!

Teacher: Little Red Riding Hood looked at them all. Gleek said, "Now Snow White will never meet her prince."

Gleek: Now Snow White will never meet her prince.

Teacher: All the fairy-tale fairies moaned in disbelief. (Fairies moan.) They could not believe she messed up another fairy tale. She said, "What? I saved her life."

Red Riding Hood: What? I saved her life.

Teacher: The fairy-tale fairies shook their heads. Two fairy tales were messed up because of Little Red Riding Hood. Gleek had to get her back to hers, and quickly. Gleek said, "We have to get you back to your story."

Gleek: We have to get you back to your story.

Teacher: Little Red Riding Hood nodded her head and said, "I just want to go to Grandma's."

Red Riding Hood: I just want to go to Grandma's.

Teacher: Gleek said, "Fine. Let's get it right this time."

Gleek: Fine. Let's get it right this time.

Teacher: Once again, Gleek hummed loudly. The fairy-tale fairies disappeared. Gleek continued to hum loudly, and that noise came back again. (Audience stamps their feet.) Little Red Riding looked around. Gleek was gone, and she was all alone again. Just then, a magical wizard crept onstage. (Stars comes onstage.) Stars looked at Little Red Riding Hood and asked, "Who are you?"

Stars: Who are you?

Teacher: Little Red Riding Hood just shook her head. Gleek had messed up again, and she was not in her fairy tale. She introduced herself, "I am Little Red Riding Hood."

Red Riding Hood: I am Little Red Riding Hood.

Teacher: Then she asked, "Where am I?"

Red Riding Hood: Where am I?

Teacher: Stars looked around to see if anyone else appeared. Then very quietly (he or she) replied, "In the Unwritten Fairy-tale Land."

Stars: In the Unwritten Fairy-tale Land.

Teacher: Little Red Riding Hood was still confused. The Unwritten Fairy-tale Land is where all the characters from unfinished stories live. Stars said, "There's no story here, just characters."

Stars: There's no story here, just characters.

Teacher: Little Red Riding Hood commented, "This is a strange land."

Red Riding Hood: This is a strange land.

Teacher: Stars said sadly, "No, just a land without a story."

Stars: No, just a land without a story.

Teacher: No story? Little Red Riding Hood could not believe that. There's a story in every fairy tale. There are good people and bad people and the good people always win. So, what was there to do here? Little Red Riding Hood began to cry. She was never going to get to Grandma's house. Stars said, "Don't cry. It will be OK."

Stars: Don't cry. It will be OK.

Teacher: Stars continued, "Your story is unfinished too, isn't it?"

Stars: Your story is unfinished too, isn't it?

Teacher: Little Red Riding Hood cried, "No, I just got lost."

Red Riding Hood: No, I just got lost.

Teacher: Stars thought about this, a story that is done. If the story is done, she should not be here. So Stars used (his or her) magical powers and shook (his or her) hands in the air. Little Red Riding Hood watched (him or her) and through her tears asked, "What are you doing?"

Red Riding Hood: What are you doing?

Teacher: Stars said, "I am going to help you. I can do magic."

Stars: I am going to help you. I can do magic."

Teacher: Stars stamped (his or her) feet three times. One, two, three. Then clapped twice. One, two. (He or she) turned around in a circle. Stars said, "Everybody help us get her to her story."

Stars: Everybody help us get her to her story.

Teacher: Stars and the audience all helped her. Everybody stamped their feet three times. One, two, three. (Audience stamps three times.) Everybody clapped twice. One, two. (Audience claps twice.) Everybody stood up and turned around and sat down. (Audience turns.) Suddenly, Stars was gone (back to audience). Little Red Riding Hood looked around. She was in a forest again. It looked like the forest from her story. She walked for a while and saw her Grandma's house. She was so excited, she said, "I'm in my story!"

Red Riding Hood: I'm in my story!

Teacher: Gleek appeared and said, "I've fixed the other stories, so everything is fine."

Gleek: I've fixed the other stories, so everything is fine.

Teacher: Little Red Riding Hood asked, "What about the Unwritten Fairy-tale Land?"

Red Riding Hood: What about the Unwritten Fairy-tale Land?

Teacher: Gleek looked confused and said, "I've never heard of it."

Gleek: I've never heard of it.

Teacher: Little Red Riding Hood was surprised. Perhaps the Unwritten Fairy-tale Land would always be a mystery. She decided to forget about it and enjoy being in her story. She opened the door to her Grandma's house and as she did, she heard that loud noise again. (Audience stamps their feet.) Gleek said, "On no, not again!"

Gleek: Oh no, not again!

The End

11
The Stolen Silver Bracelet

Play Synopsis

The Stolen Silver Bracelet is a story about honesty. Melanie steals a silver bracelet from a friend. In her dreams, she meets colorful characters such as Lies, Truth, and Trouble. Eventually, she ends up on trial for stealing and is found guilty. She awakens to realize that stealing is wrong and in the end returns the silver bracelet.

Character Descriptions

Cast size: The ideal cast size for this play is 15 students. If you have fewer than that, have the same students play multiple roles as Stacy's friends, Trouble's friends, and the jury. If you have more than that, increase the number of students playing any of the parts listed above.

Melanie is an impulsive character. Her impulse to steal gets her into all kinds of problems. This part is best played by a strong actress who can follow directions and act out a wide range of emotions—excitement, anger, disappointment, confusion, and so on.

Stacy is a quiet classmate. She does not really notice Melanie until the end of the story. Stacy is the perfect part for the student who is becoming more confident in acting and is not quite ready for a lead part but can do more than the smaller parts.

Lies and Truth are the classic opposites, like evil and good. These characters should play off each other much like the angel on one shoulder and the devil on the other shoulder. Lies convinces Melanie to do everything that is wrong, and Truth tries to convince her to do everything right.

Trouble is exactly what the name says. (He or she) is extremely mischievous and a strong leader, best played by the most extroverted student in your class.

The Judge is a distinguished person. The judge takes control of the trial scene and is best played by a student who can take this role seriously.

The Cop catches Melanie and arrests her. It is important that this role be played by someone who will not pretend to have a gun and turn the scene into a violent one. The cop's duty is to find whoever stole the money and arrest that person.

Stacy's friends are classmates. There should be a minimum of two friends.

Trouble's friends are a shady bunch. They laugh a lot and kid around with each other. They always look like they have just done something wrong. There should be a minimum of two friends.

The jury sits still and listens to the trial. They are not onstage long but play an important role in helping Melanie realize that stealing is wrong. It is their facial expressions that add life to the scene. There should be a minimum of four students playing the jury.

Characters to Use for Auditions

It is best to have students introduce themselves as characters. Describe each character before doing auditions to give students an idea of how to act. When they are onstage, remind them of how that character might speak and stand. Refer to the character descriptions above to help students. Characters to use are the following:

The Judge says, "I am the Judge."

Lies says, "I am Lies, and I tell lots of lies."

Melanie says, "My name is Melanie."

Trouble says, "I am Trouble."

Truth says, "I am Truth, and I always tell the truth."

Students who do well auditioning as Trouble or Lies but are not cast in either part can be cast as Trouble's friends. Audition for the part of the Cop but make it clear that the Cop does not have a gun. The Cop's audition is the following:

The Cop says, "Don't move."

Use the audition worksheet on the following page to make notes about your students.

Melanie

Lies

Truth

Stacy

Trouble

Judge

Cop

Trouble's friends (at least two)

Stacy's friends (at least two)

Jury (at least four)

Notes and comments:

Final Cast List

Melanie

Lies

Truth

Stacy

Trouble

Judge

Cop

Trouble's friends

Stacy's friends

Jury

Notes and comments:

Sound Effects

The following sound effects should be rehearsed before the play:

Police sirens

The bracelet hits the ground with a "clank." When it falls off Stacy's wrist, the audience must watch it fall and make the "clank" sound when it hits the ground.

When Lies enters, the audience boos. When Truth enters, the audience claps.

When Melanie falls asleep, on the teacher's cue the audience says "dream" three times. This is to distinguish reality from dream.

When Melanie gets ready for bed and for school, she brushes her teeth and washes her face. During this scene, ask the audience to make the sound effects and do these activities with her.

Remember to always use hand motions to begin and end sound effects.

Technical Aspects

There is no set for this play. When Melanie goes to sleep, she lies down on the floor. I suggest making a silver bracelet from aluminum foil and using a paper bag for Trouble and Trouble's friends to hand to Melanie. Other props that would be fun are a gavel for the Judge and a jump rope for Stacy and her friends.

Suggestions

This play is an entertaining exercise in thinking about honesty. I believe it is important to discuss what it means to steal and why it is dishonest. Ask students to think of something that they love, such as a favorite toy. Then ask them how they would feel if someone took it without asking. You'll probably get answers like "sad" and "mad." Introduce the story as one about a girl who steals and gets into a ton of trouble. It might also be useful to explain what a judge and jury do in our legal system.

The Stolen Silver Bracelet: The Play

Teacher: Melanie loved to have things. She loved having jewels. One day, some classmates started jumping rope. (Stacy and Stacy's friends come onstage.) One of them, Stacy, was wearing a shiny silver bracelet. Melanie said, "That's pretty."

Melanie: That's pretty.

Teacher: Stacy said, "Thank you."

Stacy: Thank you.

Teacher: And they jumped rope, except for Melanie. Stacy was jumping rope while her two friends turned the rope for her. While she was jumping, she was throwing her arms all over the place, up, down, and side to side. Her bracelet flew off, and she did not even notice. It made a clanking noise as it hit the ground. (Audience makes noise.) Melanie saw the bracelet but did not say anything. Stacy said, "I'm tired. Let's go."

Stacy: I'm tired. Let's go.

Teacher: And her friends agreed and they left. (Stacy and friends sit down.) Melanie stared at the bracelet. Then she picked it up and put it in her pocket. Was that the right thing to do, audience? (They all say, "No.") She went home. Later that night, she was getting ready for bed. She brushed her teeth (audience does this with her), washed her face (audience does this with her), and put on her night clothes (she pretends to slip them on). She curled up on her bed (on the floor) and went to sleep. While she was sleeping, she began to dream. (Audience quietly says, "Dream, dream, dream.") In her dream, she was still in her room and sleeping. The dream began with someone named Truth who slipped into her room. (Audience claps quietly.) Truth tapped Melanie on the shoulder and said, "Give the bracelet back."

Truth: Give the bracelet back.

Teacher: Melanie woke up quickly and asked, "Who are you?"

Melanie: Who are you?

Teacher: Truth said, "I am Truth. Give the bracelet back."

Truth: I am Truth. Give the bracelet back.

Teacher: Melanie stood up. She did not know what to say. She held the bracelet tightly in her hand. Truth said, "It is wrong to steal."

Truth: It is wrong to steal.

Teacher: Melanie angrily said, "You get out of here, now!"

Melanie: You get out of here, now!

Teacher: Before Truth could answer, Lies came in. (Audience boos.) Lies walked an evil walk. Melanie looked in disbelief at this other stranger in her room. Lies said, "Don't listen to Truth."

Lies: Don't listen to Truth.

Teacher: Truth marched over to Lies and said, "You're not needed here."

Truth: You're not needed here.

Teacher: Lies ignored Truth and walked over to Melanie. Lies said, "Come with me, and bring the bracelet."

Lies: Come with me, and bring the bracelet.

Teacher: Melanie asked, "Why?"

Melanie: Why?

Teacher: Lies laughed a evil laugh and said, "To have lots of fun adventures. Come on."

Lies: To have lots of fun adventures. Come on.

Teacher: Melanie's eyes lit up. Fun and adventure sounded great to her. Truth warned, "Don't go, Melanie."

Truth: Don't go, Melanie.

Teacher: Lies glared at Truth and took Melanie by the hand and asked, "Are you coming?"

Lies: Are you coming?

Teacher: Melanie nodded her head yes, and Truth sadly vanished (back into the audience). Melanie asked, "Where are we going?"

Melanie: Where are we going?

Teacher: Lies began to walk without speaking. Melanie followed. Lies walked (in place) and Melanie had to almost run to keep up with (him or her). Melanie asked, "Can we slow down?"

Melanie: Can we slow down?

Teacher: Lies continued to walk quickly, and Melanie continued to try to keep up. She was almost out of breath. Abruptly, Lies stopped. Melanie almost fell from stopping so quickly. Melanie whined, "This is not fun."

Melanie: This is not fun.

Teacher: Before Lies could say anything, Trouble and (his or her) gang of friends walked toward them. They were laughing. Trouble was the loudest of all, and (he or she) bellowed, "Lies, what's up?"

Trouble: Lies, what's up?

Teacher: Lies said, "Got a friend for you to meet. This is Melanie."

Lies: Got a friend for you to meet. This is Melanie.

Teacher: Melanie came forward. She was kind of scared of Trouble. (He or she) looked so mean. She said in a small voice, "Hi."

Melanie: Hi.

Teacher: Trouble and (his or her) friends laughed. Trouble said, "No need to be afraid."

Trouble: No need to be afraid.

Teacher: Melanie laughed nervously. Trouble's friends said, "Hey, check out her bracelet."

Friends: Hey, check out her bracelet.

Teacher: Lies proudly said, "She stole it."

Lies: She stole it.

Teacher: Trouble and (his or her) friends were impressed, and they all clapped. Melanie smiled. They liked her. It seemed as if they liked her even more than her classmates at school. Lies smiled proudly again and said, "Well, my work is done. Good-bye."

Lies: Well, my work is done. Good-bye.

Teacher: And Lies disappeared (back to audience). Melanie said, "Hey, wait—."

Melanie: Hey, wait—.

Teacher: But it was too late, Lies was gone. Trouble asked, "So, where did you get the bracelet?"

Trouble: So, where did you get the bracelet?

Teacher: Melanie replied, "From a classmate at school."

Melanie: From a classmate at school.

Teacher: The friends got into a huddle. Whatever they were discussing seemed very important and very secret. Trouble joined them, and Melanie tried to listen. They just kept on whispering. Finally, Trouble asked, "You want to be part of our gang?"

Trouble: You want to be part of our gang?

Teacher: Melanie said, "Sure, that would be great."

Melanie: Sure, that would be great.

Teacher: Trouble handed Melanie a huge bag and said, "Your first job is to count this."

Trouble: Your first job is to count this.

Teacher: Melanie took the huge bag and sat down. She asked, "What's in it?"

Teacher: Trouble's friends answered her and said, "Money we stole."

Friends: Money we stole.

Teacher: Melanie stared at the bag. She didn't want anything to do with stolen money. She couldn't believe it. Trouble said, "You stole a bracelet. How is that different?"

Trouble: You stole a bracelet. How is that different?

Teacher: Before Melanie could answer, they heard sirens. (Audience makes sound effect.) It was the police! Everyone scattered in all directions and disappeared from sight. (Trouble and friends go into the audience.) Melanie was the only one left. She didn't know what was going on. A Cop (no gun, just words) came running onstage and said, "Don't move!"

Cop: Don't move!

Teacher: Melanie was still sitting down, too scared to move. She looked up at the Cop and said, "I didn't do anything."

Melanie: I didn't do anything.

Teacher: The Cop looked inside the bag and saw all the money. And (he or she) saw the bracelet on Melanie's wrist. The Cop asked, "Is this money yours?"

Cop: Is this money yours?

Teacher: Without thinking, Melanie answered, "No."

Melanie: No.

Teacher: The Cop said, "You're coming with me."

Cop: You're coming with me.

Teacher: Melanie was shocked. She hadn't done anything, or at least she didn't think she had. The Cop took her to a huge room and left (into the audience). A distinguished-looking person came in. It was the Judge. (Judge comes onstage.) The Judge said, "Order, order."

Judge: Order, order.

Teacher: Melanie was confused. What was going on? She could tell she was in big trouble. Some people came into the room and sat down across from her. (Direct or move the students to their places. Melanie should be on one side, the Judge in the middle, and the jury sitting in a row facing the audience on the other side of the Judge.) These people were the jury. The Judge spoke: "You have been charged with stealing. How do you plead?"

Judge: You have been charged with stealing. How do you plead?

Teacher: Melanie asked, "How do I what?"

Melanie: How do I what?

Teacher: The Judge ignored her and reported the evidence to the jury. "She was found with stolen money."

Judge: She was found with stolen money.

Teacher: The jury members looked at Melanie and shook their heads. Stealing is wrong. The Judge asked Melanie, "Did you steal the bracelet you are wearing?"

Judge: Did you steal the bracelet you are wearing?

Teacher: Melanie squirmed a little. She looked at the bracelet and realized it had gotten her into more trouble than it was worth. She confessed, "Yes, I did."

Melanie: Yes, I did.

Teacher: The Judge asked the jury, "How do you find her, jury?"

Judge: How do you find her, jury?

Teacher: Each jury member stood up and said, "Guilty." (Point to each student so they know it is their turn to stand and say "Guilty." When the last one has said it, continue.) Melanie said, "Wait. I can explain."

Melanie: Wait. I can explain.

Teacher: The Judge said, "Guilty."

Judge: Guilty.

Teacher: The Judge drifted away (into the audience). The jury kept chanting "guilty, guilty" as they went away (into the audience). Melanie kept hearing the words "guilty, guilty, guilty."

Audience: Guilty, guilty. (Keep chanting it.)

Teacher: Melanie lay down, curled into a ball, and closed her eyes. Softly she could still hear "guilty, guilty." She sat up quickly and said, "I'll give back the bracelet."

Melanie: I'll give back the bracelet.

Teacher: The chanting stopped. She was back in her room. The whole thing was a horrible dream. She jumped out of bed and got ready for school. She put on her clothes. She walked to the bathroom and washed her face (audience does this with her), brushed her teeth (audience does this with her), and left for school. At school, Stacy and her friends were sitting down outside the school. Stacy was crying, "I can't believe my silver bracelet is gone!"

Stacy: I can't believe my silver bracelet is gone!

Teacher: Melanie walked over to them and handed Stacy her silver bracelet. Melanie said, "You dropped this yesterday, and I took it."

Melanie: You dropped this yesterday, and I took it.

Teacher: Stacy looked surprised. She took the bracelet back and put it on. Melanie said, "I'm really sorry. I'll never ever steal again."

Melanie: I'm really sorry. I'll never ever steal again.

Teacher: Melanie assumed that Stacy would be furious. She began to walk away from them (Melanie begins to leave). Stacy said, "Wait. I'm glad you gave it back."

Stacy: Wait. I'm glad you gave it back.

Teacher: Melanie stopped. She could not believe that Stacy said to wait. Stacy thought for a few moments. She was upset that Melanie stole her silver bracelet, but she decided to forgive her. She said, "Let's forget about it. Want to play?"

Stacy: Let's forget about it. Want to play?

Teacher: Melanie said, "Sure, I'd love to."

Melanie: Sure, I'd love to.

Teacher: And they all played together, and Melanie never stole or lied again.

The End

Conclusion

I hope you find this book to be useful to you and your students. With each performance, students will develop their acting skills. For further activities, take your favorite story and turn it into a play. Students can act out scenes from the book as you tell the story. If there are not enough parts for everyone, have different students play different parts each time you tell the story. This way, students are not just listening to a story, they are a part of it. To add more parts to the same story, ask your students for advice. You will be surprised at how creative children can be when they brainstorm together.

Bringing theatre into the classroom has always been a rewarding experience for me. I hope you find this no-script format to be easy and fun to use. Theatre is a valuable educational tool, as well as a great resource in building children's self-confidence and self-esteem. Your students will benefit greatly from your decision to use theatre in the classroom.